The
Power
of
Positive
Productivity

Accelerate Your Success and Create the Life You Want

Dennis E. Hensley, Ph.D.

A *Possibility Press* Book

The
Power
of
Positive
Productivity

Accelerate Your Success and Create the Life You Want

Dennis E. Hensley, Ph.D.

Copyright © 2008 by Dennis E. Hensley, Ph.D.
ISBN 13: 978-0-938716-53-2
ISBN 10: 0-938716-53-0

1   2   3   4   5   6   7   8   9   10

Published by
Possibility Press
info@possibilitypress.com

Dedication

This book is affectionately dedicated to my son Nathan, in special recognition of the completion of his MBA degree in entrepreneurship from Ball State University. This is also to honor him for all the good he has done and is doing as a United States Marine, a successful businessman, and a member of our family.

Contents

"I *always felt spe-cial because my daddy worked at home. I could see him any-time I wanted to, really. Other kids' fathers were gone all day, but not my dad... having him there felt good."*

—Jeanette M. Hensley

I Always Felt Special Because My Daddy Worked at Home

I could see my daddy anytime I wanted to, really. Other kids' fathers were gone all day, but not *my* dad. Of course, there were times my brother and I weren't allowed to disturb him. So my mother ingeniously thought of putting a red circle sign on his door when he needed to be alone; the flip side was green, giving the "all clear" warm welcome we treasured. But just having him there felt good, regardless of the color of the circle. (I fondly remember going into his office and quietly drawing pictures with his colored pens.)

He happily worked all hours of the day and night, but he always pulled himself away to eat dinner with the family. And because he made his own schedule, he never missed one of my school plays or choir concerts. He was always there for birthdays, was a leader in my brother's boys youth group, and even played adult roles in our church's children's Christmas plays.

Dad traveled quite a bit—and most of the time he took us with him! During the school year, we'd spend Friday nights in hotels where he was speaking on Saturdays. In the summers, it was week-long trips to Wisconsin, Florida, and everywhere in between. Because of my dad's work, I traveled a lot more than most kids my age. And I thought it was great!

Considerable time has passed since then. I am now an adult, and I've taken on a lot of my father's positive productivity-related characteristics. I use my time wisely. I like being organized and enjoy solitude when I'm working. I've also developed his love of travel, having already been to more than half of the 50 states and several other countries. I've taken the teaching legacy from both of my parents a generation further, with my own teaching career. And, like my dad, I love being productive. I just wouldn't have it any other way.

Warmest wishes,

Jeanette M. Hensley

"*Just like everyone else, I have my share of challenges. However, I'm different in one respect: I usually accomplish more in one year than others accomplish in three. Why? I'm a positive producer and I love it.*"

—Dennis E. Hensley

Understanding the Power of Positive Productivity

"The power of positive productivity, when used to give meaning to one's life, to serve others, and to provide security and enjoyment to one's family and self, is something to aspire to every day."
—Dennis E. Hensley—

"Hello, my name is Dennis…and I am a positive producer." And I don't drink, smoke, swear, or gamble. Now don't get me wrong. I'm not saying this because I think I'm better or more righteous than anyone else—I'm just busier than most and I have neither the time nor the inclination for such negative habits.

Granted, you could find plenty of people who would look at my life and point to habits of mine which might seem odd. For example, I seldom sleep more than six hours a night. I refuse to go on vacations that last more than five days. And I'm efficient and focused in my business activities—I don't like wasting time. I can't seem to do anything nonproductive "just for the fun of it" because, truth be told, my work is my fun!

Choose to be a participant in life, not just a spectator. We're all here to make a difference, not just sit on the sidelines and be entertained.

Just like everyone else, I have my share of challenges. However, I'm different in one respect: I usually accomplish more in one year than others accomplish in three. Why? I'm a positive producer and I love it.

I left my parents' home in 1970 when I was 22 years old, just after finishing college. Since then, I have served two years in the U.S. Army, earned M.A. and Ph.D. degrees, got married, became a father and helped raise two children, wrote voraciously, including, among other things, more than 3,000 freelance articles, traveled to Asia, the South Seas, Europe, the Caribbean, and across America, became the owner of rental properties and other real estate holdings, was a guest lecturer at more than 60 colleges and universities, made appearances on numerous TV and radio talk shows, served more than 20 years as a church deacon and Sunday school teacher, taught English at the university level for many years, served as a staff columnist for five national magazines, and worked four years as a top-level member of a public relations department at an old-line college in the Midwest. I'm not telling you all of this to brag, but simply to say that I love to accomplish worthwhile goals.

Being a positive producer is a powerful force in my life. It gives me incentive, direction, purpose, drive, ambition, and a friendly competitive spirit. It also earns me recognition, gives me financial security, and provides all the niceties of life for me and my family.

Furthermore, I believe I do good work and that I'm a useful member of society—I contribute to it. I've been told that my writing teaches and entertains, and that my presentations provide hope and motivation. As an author, I do my best to share experiences, new approaches, and improved techniques, and according to the feedback I get, I believe I am helping others. I'm happy with who I am and what I do. I've even been told that my work is honest, helpful, and practical—and appreciated by others. I believe I live a great life, and you can too.

The world needs more positive producers. Before the age of the push-button society, the ability to work was something admired in a person, even expected. The Apostle Paul wrote in 54 A.D: "If any would not work, neither should he eat." A millennium-and-a-half later, in the 1600s, Captain John Smith instituted the same law when he and his followers set about to build a colony in New England.

Somewhere along the way, however, this basic belief, among many others, has been diluted. The more entitlement programs there are, the more people there are who will adopt the free-ride philosophy in place of the honest, hardwork approach to success.

In the U.S., a dear price has been paid for this change in attitude. Well-organized, ambitious, creative industrial nations now more competitively provide the world's steel, automotive, and electronic markets, while OPEC nations control a majority of the world's oil. Other countries are even providing more of the world's produce. The U.S. has lost some of its edge in world markets.

While people in the U.S. were talking about the need for a four-day workweek, longer vacations with pay, earlier retirements, and lower work quotas, they lost customers to those who rolled up their sleeves and worked harder. The work ethic grew weak and, as a result, people suffered.

Positive producers, as individuals, however, never suffer. They are generally too independent to be part of a labor union; hence, they seldom lose money because of strikes or layoffs. They are too ambitious to be limited by quotas or have goals set for them by someone else. They set their own goals, and make them high. They then go out and do whatever it takes to reach them, and reap the rich rewards and other fine benefits the achievement of such goals provides.

Positive producers are strategists. They make their own game plans in life. They always know the score, too, whether it's kick-off, halftime, or the final play. No one catches positive producers off-guard. They always have a mentor or leader and a support group—people they can rely on—and a proven system of success for themselves and others to follow.

Positive producers are unmoved by and certainly not impressed with polls, trends, indicators, naysayers, or fads. Instead, they are doggedly bent on reaching their own personal goals. Whatever or whomever the masses choose to follow is of no concern to them; positive producers always maintain a single vision of personal direction. They thrive on being unique, influential, purposeful, and productive. Positive producers are masters of their own destinies.

The positive producer is not one to say, "Thank goodness it's Friday," because one day is as precious, important, and eventful as the next. In fact, the positive producer is always "on" regarding his work or mission. Famed author W. Somerset Maugham was once asked by a reporter how he had been able to write so many plays, short stories, and novels when it was known he spent only three hours a day working. "Young man," replied Maugham, "I *write* twenty-four hours a day; I only *type* three hours a day."

Researchers believe that only one person in four is a genuine positive producer. But being an exhausted, worn-out worker is not the same as being a positive producer. Clergymen and psychiatrists hear confessions from so-called positive producers who, in reality, are simply disorganized crybabies. Unfortunately, since the overworked, disorganized person is the first (and often loudest) person to complain, his or her traumatized condition is often held up as an example of the end-product of productivity. But the genuine positive producer doesn't need to visit a counselor. He or she just wouldn't feel comfortable lying down on a couch in the middle of the day!

Work helps define our sense of self-worth. If we feel we are doing good work and being appreciated by others, we also feel good about ourselves; we have a positive sense of self-worth. But there are many reasons why positive producers might be viewed in a negative way. Some people tend to put down or criticize those who are more successful than they are. Yes, jealousy does exist. And, unfortunately, it can lead to negative remarks from less ambitious people about the positive producer's lifestyle and work patterns. Honest, hardworking people have become such a rare breed that they are often looked upon as suspicious characters. This usually leads to distrust and perhaps even harassment—until the consistency of a positive producer's fine character and success wins the doubters over.

The world needs people with spunk, energy, ambition, and a great work ethic, even though some put this down. Many of the critic's ideas stem from the best of intentions. They want to help people better deal with stress or reevaluate their lives, or learn to be less apprehensive about life's challenges. Nevertheless, these ideas often serve only as an excuse from the reality that people generally identify themselves, to a large extent, with the work they do and the things they accomplish.

Consider how introductions are often made. After someone learns your name, that person usually asks, "And what line of work are you in?" or "Who are you with?" This is why some people feel greatly alienated after they retire; they have been separated from their jobs or businesses and their life's identities. No matter how much we may joke or complain about it, we all need to be doing some kind of productive work. It gives us a sense of purpose and a feeling that we can make a difference. To fail at one's work is to fail at achieving security, recognition, money, respect, and responsibility. Nothing can hide the power of positive productivity.

This book presents a counterargument to those who espouse that steady, challenging work is something negative and needs to be avoided. We'll explode that myth, and you'll learn how you can work at an incredible pace, yet stay in excellent health, enjoy your family, remain highly respected in your community, and be happier about who you are and what you are doing.

Unfortunately, there are people who are so preoccupied and obsessive about their work that they eventually become nervous wrecks. They can't say no to anyone; they are unable to relax; and they are afraid they won't be able to measure up to some obscure standard they believe others have set for them. These people, much like drug addicts or alcoholics, need professional help. They are not normal; and, in truth, they *are* suffering. The harried worker on the verge of a nervous breakdown is not a positive producer.

Positive Productivity is gratifying. It gives meaning to life, a greater opportunity to serve others, and provides increased security and enjoyment for our families and ourselves. And those are just some of the many benefits of being a positive producer.

Take a long, hard look at your own personal work ethic and productivity. If you'd like to improve upon them, this book can help you do so. If you are not happy with your current productivity, you'll learn the tips and techniques needed to change it.

We'll examine the traits of positively productive people and why many of them gravitate toward independent business ownership. We'll also evaluate some of the published commentaries on stress to see if they are accurate about a person's capacity for sustained work. In addition, we'll also look at the benefits to be gained by becoming a positive producer, and explore ways in which you can maintain your newly established productive pace—without sacrificing any important aspects of your social, family, and religious commitments. If you are at a stage in life where you want to accomplish more, earn more, and be needed and respected more, then this book could be the beacon to guide you out of the storm of just-being-busy frustration.

Working simply for the sake of working is a waste of human potential—just ask anyone who has worked hard and not gotten anywhere. It's all too easy to be busy and broke, no matter what field you may be in. But working for the sake of advancing yourself and the society you live in will have a positive effect on you and those around you. There's a big difference between simply being busy and being a positive producer.

There is a proverb that says, "He who plows and plows but never plants seed does not reap." This book shows you how to plant the seeds of leadership skills, sound work practices, and building positive human relations, which will grow and bear fruit when you invest time in nurturing them. That's positive productivity, and that's what this book is all about.

To gain an overview of the qualities of a positive producer, take a look at *The Positive Producer—At a Glance* on the next page.

The Positive Producer
—At a Glance

> - Open-Minded
> - Extremely Fair
> - Always Learning
> - Innovative
> - Resourceful

AMBITIOUS
ORGANIZED
CONFIDENT
CARING
EAGER & ENERGETIC
SECURE
COMPETITIVE
MOTIVATED
USEFUL & HELPFUL
HAPPY & JOYFUL
PROGRESSIVE
A TEAM PLAYER

> - A Servant Leader
> - A Self-Starter
> - A Challenge-
>   Overcomer
> - A Dedicated Worker

"*Choose to be a participant in life, not just a spectator. We're all here to make a difference, not just sit on the sidelines and be entertained.*"

—Dennis E. Hensley

"*In a free enterprise system, we are limited only by the size of our dreams and the amount of work and number of positive producers we put into our organizations.*"

—Dennis E. Hensley

—1—
Developing an Art of Work

*"People who really dig into their work,
without being concerned about their current circumstances
or the outcome, are the ones who later
reap rich rewards."*
—Dennis E. Hensley—

For several years I worked as editor-in-chief of a magazine for graduates of a small, mid-western college. From time to time, the editorial board and I would poll our readers to discover what they liked best about our publication—our front-page articles, feature stories, the photographs we ran, our sports reports, or our ads. The results of these surveys always came back to us with the same opening response, phrased in one form or another: "My favorite section of your magazine is the last page, where the alumni news is printed."

I've talked with dozens of other editors of college magazines, and they've told me their surveys elicit the same response. Why is this? People simply want to see what their old friends have accomplished in life and learn about the contributions they've made so far. Perhaps this will inspire them to do more than they've already done.

If you are in the habit of reading your college alumni news, or if you've ever picked up one of those "Where Are They Now?" booklets at your high school class reunions, you've probably already discovered something interesting. Although everyone listed had a similar beginning (same age and graduation year, and many of the same teachers), no two lived identical lives, nor did they achieve the same levels of success and hapiness!

For example, you observe that of the two boys who were co-captains of the football team, one is a successful business owner who loves what he does and works long hours at it. The other is a construction worker, who, compared to many people, earns very good money, but he hates the work and, therefore, won't put in the extra hours to move up in his occupation. Of the two girls who graduated at the head of the class, one is a doctor who loves helping people. The other is a corporate manager who's anxious to leave the office every day. Of your two closest friends, one is a disgruntled vice president of a computer company, while the other became a happy piano teacher.

Why are there such vast differences in the outcomes? Why is there such a tremendous variation in the levels of happiness and success? Why would there be such a wide range of achievement?

Sure, all of your friends may be working and supporting themselves and serving society in useful occupations. But how have some of them been able to gain wealth, influence, personal freedom, and happiness, while others seemingly have had to settle for routine jobs and run-of-the-mill lives? Simply put: *Each person had a different attitude toward work, and that's what has largely shaped his or her life.*

We all want to be successful and happy, and some of us want to be more influential, so we can make more of a difference. "Every human being with a healthy will to live has a natural drive for power, a drive that goes beyond his need for mere survival," says Dr. Arnold A. Hutschnecker, M.D. "It is an urge to unfold as much of his inert potentials as his courage will allow, and a wish to gain recognition that aims to give back to the world what he has received from it, possibly more."

However, fulfilling that drive requires hard work. The typical saga is the challenging story of super-achievers—people who were convinced they could accomplish anything if they were given enough freedom in which to do their work. Even folk heroes like John Henry, Pecos Bill, and Paul Bunyan were all people of strength, whether a "steel drivin' man" or a giant lumberjack. We've always admired those who could roll up their sleeves, dig in, get their hands dirty, and achieve the seemingly impossible.

As Dr. Hutschnecker puts it, "...Today's culture sets a high priority on achievement. The need to excel is a conditioned process deeply ingrained in us from childhood. The philosophy of 'making good' is evident as a driving force in a society that has coined the phrase 'the sky's the limit.'"

We observe our former classmates and current peers with curious interest and we are eager to know who is making good and who is not. Many times, unfortunately, by comparison, we are also ranking and judging ourselves—probably putting ourselves down, which is only self-discouraging. The question you need to ask of yourself is, "Am I growing and accomplishing more than ever before?" Compare yourself only with yourself.

An Attitude Toward Work—*You Need to Love It!*

In a free enterprise system, we are limited only by the size of our dreams, and the amount of work and number of positive producers we put into our organizations. For example, just walk into the doorway of the Henry Ford Museum in Greenfield Village, Dearborn, Michigan, and glance at the huge photo on the wall. Seated around a campsite are three friends: Harvey Firestone, Thomas Edison, and Henry Ford. Each had been a poor boy with a burning desire and a tremendous love of hard work, while being smart enough to leverage with others. As a result, they all became industrial magnates worth millions.

Men like Firestone, Edison, and Ford had the same natural desire for success and influence that you and I have. They knew what they wanted, and they were willing to work with passion to get it. They were the real-life "steel drivin' men." And, thanks to their efforts, many of us were given a better way of life. They certainly gave back more to the world than they ever received from it.

But in providing all of us a better way of life, these industrial giants also did something subtle, yet monumental, to society's work ethic. The cars, airplanes, light bulbs, tires, assembly lines, and laborsaving devices they created gave the world something it never had before—easier or more comfortable ways to travel and accomplish other things. And we do rather enjoy it.

In fact, various innovators did all they could to manufacture more creature comforts. Electric vacuum cleaners made broom sweeping a thing of the past; refrigerators did away with handling ice; telephones and the internet allowed for instant communication; and gas and electric ranges and microwave ovens forever put an end to chopping wood for cooking stoves.

Along with the influx of these laborsaving devices, a new attitude was developed about enjoying an easier life. The most frequently heard phrases after World War II were, "It's gonna be better for my kid. He's not going to have to work the way I always had to. He's gettin' an education. He'll have 'the good life.'"

And so it was that many of us who grew up in the 1950s—my generation—were *given* way too many things. We didn't work to earn money to buy our toys; we were *given* toys. We got them on our birthdays, at holidays, at school report card time, as rewards for sitting quietly during religious services. And some of us even got our way just because we saw a toy in a department store window and threw a tantrum until our parents gave in and bought it. Before too long, we began feeling that we were entitled to even bigger things.

Back then, we didn't worry about paying for things. We knew Dad worked *somewhere* and he seemed happy; so we let his money pay our way. It was a great life...until we graduated from high school or college and were told that we needed to find a job.

"What! Work?" we protested. "You've got to be kidding! We don't work; we receive. That's what you've reared us to do."

But told to work we were. And, as always, when we weren't given our toys, or our livelihood, on a silver platter, we threw a tantrum. Back in the mid-to-late 1960s, we marched with signs, tore up college campuses, burned military draft cards, grew our hair long, and called law enforcement officers unkind names. Some of us even ran off to hide away in communes in other countries.

So, what was gained by this rebellion against the traditional work ethic? Where are we now? It's the 21st century and we're experiencing fluctuating unemployment, slow economic growth, stock market reactions, and dangerous lows in productivity. By letting our work muscles get flabby, we've allowed others to challenge our championship rankings.

Regrouping—*Strengthening the Work Ethic*

According to the dictionary, work ethic refers to a belief in the moral benefit and importance of work, and its inherent ability to strengthen character.

Fortunately, at least in some areas, things are beginning to show signs of swinging back toward an honest day's work for an honest day's pay. Some unions are accepting cuts in their current contracts to avoid further layoffs. Lawyers are advertising their services in direct competition with each other, and some are reducing their high fees to remain competitive. Some young doctors are doing house calls; a number of recently ordained ministers are not charging fees above their salaries for weddings and funerals; and there are teachers who are volunteering to sponsor student activities without asking for a raise or "released" time.

These are positive steps, but they remain more rarities than common practice. A great many people remain who are still depending upon others to watch out for them or to do their share of the difficult work. They've forgotten or, perhaps, never knew how to work hard and be independent. About 25 percent of the people have not forgotten how to work hard, nor have they lost any of their self-respect or control of their personal lives. They are the positive producers. They are working hard, enjoying every minute of it and, as a result, living a better life.

"Enjoying it?" you ask.

Yes, that's right. Not only are they enjoying what they are doing, they are also helping society advance. It's a great system.

"But...but I've heard that people who work a lot are neurotic," some may respond.

You may be aware of the claims being made by some so-called experts in the field who say that hard workers are mentally ill, copping-out on life, or are engaging in an escapist's fantasy…and any number of other negative descriptions. But what they are really talking about is extremism, or those who might better be called negative producers—people who are frantic and way out of balance—who harm their marriages and family lives because of their obsession with work. Some call them workaholics, which is not a healthy or happy state in which to be. I am not denying that such a condition can develop; my argument, however, is that negative labeling for all people whose habit is to work a lot is both misleading and incorrect. All the successful people I know or have read about are positive producers.

My father founded three companies—an artificial eye laboratory, a contact lens company, and a traditional eyeglasses business—and he was president of all three simultaneously. He certainly didn't do it by watching TV! In fact, he still had time to be our scout leader, coach our ball teams, run the church's orphan care fund, and serve as president of the local Optimist Club. He was a balanced, well-organized, positive producer, but definitely not frantic.

John Drake, author and work ethic consultant, perfectly describes today's frustrated worker. He says this person is working for someone else; he or she is someone who never leaves the office on time and has incredible feelings of anger built up inside. Drake confesses that this was a profile of himself until he resigned from his job at a giant human resources consulting firm, moved to Maine, and started his own business.

Yes, being a positive producer working for someone else can, indeed, be a frustrating experience. It doesn't give the worker a chance to control matters, increase personal income beyond a certain point, or change lives to the magnitude an expansive business owner can. However, this does not imply that hard work, in and of itself, is bad. Quite frankly, I would have quit Drake's job and gone out on my own too. I admire him for that.

The 25 percent of people who qualify as positive producers would probably feel the same way I do. A positive producer is someone who believes in a positive work ethic. That person's foundational belief is that hard work is good for the individual, his or her family, and the society in which the producer lives and to which he or she contributes.

Some researchers have actually discovered that hard work is something that helps keep people healthy. In a feature article titled "Bored to Sickness" in *Psychology Today* magazine, it was noted that men who worked 55 or more hours a week were in much better health than those who worked a standard 40-hour workweek. For example, physicians who worked 55-70 hours a week were far healthier than unionized assembly line workers who put in only 40 hours.

"Despite the burden," reported *Psychology Today*, "doctors were most satisfied with their work. They ranked low in depression, anxiety, and irritation, and reported few cases of poor appetite, insomnia, or similar stress-related physical problems. Assembly-line workers were at the other extreme. Most of them worked normal hours at a regular pace and had little responsibility. Yet, they were the least satisfied with their workload and they complained about depression, poor appetite, insomnia, and other physical problems."

The article cited research done by the University of Michigan which proved that, more important than workload, pressure, and other external factors, job satisfaction appeared to be the key in keeping workers healthy. The positive producer is healthy, whereas the person working at a monotonous job is a more likely candidate to be wearing the label "neurotic."

If these researchers are correct—and I'm convinced they are—we then see that the key to a good work record is job satisfaction. And the keys to good health and personal happiness are linked to job satisfaction too.

But how do we know whether we are satisfied with our career or business? If we earn enough money to emulate the people seen in television commercials, doesn't that imply we are satisfied? The people in the commercials seem to be satisfied; and since we brush with the same kind of toothpaste they do, drink the same brand of coffee, wash with the same soap, wear the same watches, drive the same cars, and sneeze into the same kind of tissues, shouldn't we be as satisfied as they seem to be? Well, if you think so, there's an "oceanfront" property in Arizona on which I'd like to quote you a good price!

No, career or business satisfaction cannot be measured simply by income. In fact, the variables that determine satisfaction are so diverse from person to person that only you can judge for yourself how satisfying your career or business is. So sit down with a pen and a clean sheet of paper and make an analysis summary of your current career or business.

Analyzing Your Potential—*for Success*

The 16 questions below will help you begin seriously evaluating both yourself and your attitude toward your career or business—whether you work for someone else or yourself—and your personal development. You can think of more personalized questions to add to the list as you go along.

1. Are you staying current in your field? **Yes No**

2. Do you anticipate and plan for change? **Yes No**

3. Do you accept constructive criticism? **Yes No**

4. Do you have a personal work ethic? **Yes No**

5. Are you a disciplined worker? **Yes No**

6. Do you use common sense in making decisions? **Yes No**

7. Do you keep expanding the inventory of your personal skills? **Yes No**

8. Are you confident in all that you do? **Yes No**

9. Do you maintain excellent health? **Yes No**

10. Are you ethical in your business practices? **Yes No**

11. Do your colleagues respect you? **Yes No**

12. Have you made a contingency plan for your income development and long-term family security? **Yes No**

13. Are you making use of all available resources to advance your career or business? **Yes No**

14. Do you continually challenge yourself with new dreams, goals, quotas, objectives, and career or business targets? **Yes No**

15. Have you learned what kinds of incentives you need to spur you on to work harder? **Yes No**

16. Can you handle pressure by facing up to challenges and then overcoming them in a systematic way? **Yes No**

If you answered yes to nine of the questions, you are about average; if you said yes to 12 or more questions, you are well on your way to enjoying a successful life and career or business. By being honest with yourself, you will learn why you may not be giving that extra effort or why you are not measuring up to your performance potential. In some instances, you may discover that you lack the right kind of motivation, don't have big enough dreams and goals, or that you are too complacent in your willingness to give it your all. These are all "curable" challenges. But before you endeavor to repair the individual *parts*, you first need to evaluate the *whole*; namely, your basic concept of a work ethic.

A Personal Work Ethic—*You Need One to Win in Life*

It's obviously ethical to do good work. Conversely, to accept payment for a job or business activity which is done in a slipshod manner could actually be cheating or stealing and, thus, unethical.

Accepting full payment for a halfway effort puts one into a position of bilking his or her employer, associates, or clients. But have you ever considered how it may also be cheating the cheater as well? I'll illustrate this by sharing an ancient Arabian fable:

> Three riders were crossing the desert one night when they lost their way. They came upon a dry riverbed and began crossing it, when a mysterious voice from out of the darkness sternly announced, "Halt and dismount!" So, cautiously, the riders climbed down. The voice then ordered them to reach into the sandy riverbed to dig out some stones and place them inside their saddlebags. Each man reached down and picked up a few stones, following the orders.
>
> The voice then said, "Now, ride away. Tomorrow, when you recall this event, it will be both the happiest and the saddest moment in your lives."
>
> The riders remounted and dashed away. At dawn, they reached an oasis where they drank water and bathed. Feeling refreshed, they went to throw the dirty rocks out of their saddlebags. To their amazement, they discovered the stones had miraculously turned into diamonds!
>
> The men leaped for joy and began dancing around ecstatically. Then, suddenly, one man stopped. His face turned grim. He held up a hand for silence and said, "Why are we joyful, brothers? We are fools! Last night we had a chance to scoop up many pounds of stones. We could have filled our saddlebags. Instead, we settled for these few stones in our hands. We have missed a chance to become rich beyond all comprehension."

This fable has much to say about life and work. People who really dig into their work, doing the best they can, without being concerned about the current circumstances or attached to the outcome, are the ones who later reap rich rewards. Positive producers are always digging up as many stones as they can, by reading positive books, working more, meeting new people, prospecting new business, and helping others. In time, those "stones" will become "diamonds" like career advancement, business expansion, public recognition, and financial gain.

The eagerness to work first and then look forward to rewards later, stems from a personal work ethic that defines the natural value of work. As with analyzing yourself and your attitude toward your career or business, analyzing your work ethic also needs to be determined on a personal basis.

Perhaps you've always assumed you had an understanding of your own work ethic. But this may not be entirely the case. Instead of just assuming this, go ahead and take a moment now to write down what you really think a fair and *honest* work performance would be. After that, define a job or business that would enable you to best contribute to society, while making your dreams come true. Next, explain how you feel the *value* of your work needs to be determined and evaluated. Finally, make a note of the opportunities available to you that offer you chances to fulfill the work ethic standards you have just set.

Establishing a Stronger Personal Work Ethic

Begin by completing the following four sentences.

1. To me, honest work is work that…. Honesty. hours

2. To me, respectable work is work that… enth mile, Love what y

3. To me, valuable work is work that…. Financial value Do.

4. To me, my ideal career or business offers me…. AR Financial Freedom

30

Once you've established a stronger personal work ethic, you will start living up to it and excelling more. The moment you do, you will have taken the first step toward a life of positive productivity. The things you accomplish will be symbolic works of art. You will have developed *an art of work*.

Living a Truly Rewarding Life

Some people may appear to be competitive, want you to think they are the stars of the class reunion, and pretend to have the good life for themselves and their families—often based on a heavy debt load and intense dissatisfaction. Unfortunately, many of them have forgotten that being truly happy and successful requires work—sustained, do-whatever-it-takes, persistent effort. Living a truly rich and rewarding life and achieving financial freedom doesn't come for free!

In my parent's generation, there was more of an emphasis on hard work. But the more advanced society became, the more complacent its people seemed to become. And they distanced themselves from understanding the need for continuous hard work. As a result, this laxity has caused some economic and social challenges.

The solution lies in a rekindling of the work ethic worldwide and it all begins with you and me on an individual basis. We need to rekindle it for ourselves and be sterling examples for others to follow. So let's get started!

"**B**ut the positive producer isn't just a blind follower! He or she is more likely to own a business, be in charge of at least part of the operation, or be in training for a leadership role."

—Dennis E. Hensley

—2—

Positive Producers Can Excel and Receive Great Rewards When They Build Their Own Businesses

*"It's 9-to-5 to survive, but
after 5 to thrive."*
—Unknown—

A ll your life you've probably heard that catch phrase about the blind leading the blind. Let me show you how that might apply to you if you are not already fully committed to your independence as an independent business owner.

In Jack London's short story "The Stampede to Squaw Creek," he gives a graphic display of how the blind can lead the blind to destruction. London's story is set in the Yukon during the great Gold Rush of 1898. Literally thousands of men had gone to the Far North to find wealth in the gold fields, but only a few actually became bonanza kings. Nevertheless, each time one man struck a rich vein of gold, it spurred thousands of other get-rich-quick neophytes to stay on and keep searching.

Late one night, Smoke Bellew, a prospector in Dawson, got a tip that gold had been discovered at Squaw Creek, several miles north of town. Instantly, Bellew hurried to his cabin and woke his partner. He told him to quickly get dressed so that they could quietly sneak out of town, get to Squaw Creek, and stake their claims before the word got out about the newly discovered gold.

The two men raced to the edge of town, only to discover that word of the strike had already spread like wildfire. Hundreds of men carrying picks, shovels, and torches were strung out in a long line heading toward Squaw Creek. They were following Louis Gastell, a native of the region, because he could break a trail even in the darkness.

Bellew and his partner got in line too. And even though the Arctic air cut their faces, numbed their hands and toes, and chilled their lungs, they continued to tread forward. As the day progressed, Bellew and his buddy spotted a woman who had fallen through some ice. They got out of line, stopped to rescue her, and stayed to build her a fire. But this delay allowed all of the other gold hunters to get miles ahead of them. Their chances for catching up and establishing claim sites were gone.

At that point, the woman finally revealed her identity. She was Joy Gastell, daughter of Louis, the pathfinder. She told Bellew and his partner some shocking news. Her father was not going to Squaw Creek after all, and, in fact, never said he was. He had just walked out of Dawson and was followed by every novice who saw him! But old Louis was walking in the wrong direction. He wanted to be sure that his friends, the old prospectors of Dawson, had time to get to Squaw Creek so they could stake all the good sites for themselves.

Later, as Bellew returned to Dawson, he passed the dead and frozen bodies of dozens of misguided beginners who had blindly followed a stranger...simply because everyone else had been doing so. They had followed the wrong leader and died, all the while thinking they were on the trail to guaranteed wealth.

This scenario brings many questions to mind: Why wasn't anyone independent-thinking enough to use a compass and map and then say, "Hey, this isn't the right direction"? Why didn't the men take along food, blankets, matches, and tents, rather than just digging equipment? Why didn't anyone say, "If the masses are going to that one creek, isn't this my big chance to get to a different area and be the first to discover gold there"?

No one asked any of these questions. And that's what makes the story so real, so believable. People frequently act that way in various areas of life. Most folks want someone else to take the risk and blaze the trail, while they remain content to tag along behind. You find such people on assembly lines in large factories, all dressed in look-alike clothes, and all doing exactly what the person next to them is doing—going nowhere fast. You find them in any number of careers, all working at similar tasks and all following the leader at the head of the "line."

But the positive producer isn't just a blind follower! He or she is more likely to own a business, be in charge of at least part of the operation, or be in training for a leadership role. Positive producers have a need to express themselves and be who they are, and the opportunity to take the lead and show what they can do. They can't hide their traits. Even if you were to require that they wear the same uniform, you would find the positive producer has his or her own personality and distinctive style. They don't follow the crowd. They won't be limited by a wage with a cap on it, a job with a ceiling, or anything that holds them back from realizing their full potential.

To a positive producer, the wonderful thing about being an independent business owner is that there is always the opportunity to do something more that he or she *wants* to do. A secretary has prescribed duties to perform; a mail carrier has a route to cover; a factory worker has a shift's worth of work to complete; and a truck driver has a shipment to deliver. An employee has duties he or she *must* perform and generally a preset schedule or number of hours to work to keep the job. He or she is trading time for money. But the independent business owner chooses what to do and can change that choice if he or she decides on a different goal or path in life. About 5 percent of the population, all of them positive producers, achieves great financial success by carrying out their choices. And many of them go on to reap even more incredible monetary rewards.

Positive producers *love* to work and accomplish things, and they love seeing results. They are do-whatever-it-takes people who are passionate about what they're doing. They'd often rather work than relax, sit down, and take it easy. They tell themselves, "That's enough," when *they* are good and ready to do so because they are their own bosses.

Stress pioneer Dr. William Glasser, M.D. feels, as I do, that positive producers excel in business because they want to accomplish more than most others. Dr. Glasser calls this a positive addiction. He says that "They win...and some win big...." In further defining the drive of the positive producer, Dr. Glasser explains that "a positive addiction is something people choose to do, physical or mental. They believe it has some value for them, and it is something they can do on their own." It's the lure of taking charge of their destiny that woos positive producers to business ownership.

Other researchers support the theory that positive producers have an addiction to succeeding and accomplishing. Author Mary Alice Kellogg said, "One all-important quality separates the doers from the drifters—*the need to achieve.* Such people *must* achieve, and they are driven by an intense need to be Somebody. Drive is the most important of the myriad qualities needed to achieve. Drive is the peculiar hunger to extend oneself, to test oneself constantly, to excel. Thus, drive is the starting point."

Kellogg says that because positive producers have this incredible drive, many cannot be content with an employment situation. They must have the freedom to set their own ceilings of success. As she puts it, "Some of these young successes..., over-workers or not, genuinely like to work hard and are uncomfortable when they cannot. Treading water just isn't in their nature."

This, obviously, goes against society's typical concept of work, the 40-hour workweek, which has long been accepted as the standard of productivity. Most people are content with that. After all, it's what everyone else does, right?

Well, not *everyone.*

For instance, consider that there are 168 hours in a week (24 x 7). If you sleep 8 hours a day, that takes up 56 hours. If you spend 40 hours at your job, and 2 hours traveling to and from it, that brings the total to 106 hours. Subtract those 106 planned-for hours from the total 168 hours, and you discover that you still have 62 hours a week left to do with as you choose.

That's pretty amazing, isn't it? This means that if you worked *two* full-time 40-hour-a-week jobs, you would still be able to sleep 8 hours a day and also have 22 hours to do with as you decide. The positive producer sees this and realizes its potential. "Why," he or she asks, "would I be content with a mere 40 hours of productive effort just because someone else said that was adequate? No, I think I'll step off that trail, check my own life maps and career or business compasses, and then blaze my own trail. I'm not going to follow anyone in the wrong direction!"

Many people who are unhappily engaged in the 40-hour routine often find themselves surfing the Internet, watching endless hours of TV, reading thriller or romance novels, or going to the movies to distract and entertain themselves, often wasting time. They simply don't love what they do or dislike some aspect of it. They waste away their non-working hours instead of investing time in being productive. Quality moments of their lives are being squandered rather than savored.

Two out of three people who log a typical work week are so bored, unfulfilled, and dissatisfied with their jobs that they participate in nonproductive activities in an attempt to "escape" a situation they don't like. But escapism only masks the boredom which can sometimes lead to depression. Getting a good paycheck simply can't make up for doing something they'd just as soon not do for someone they'd just as soon not do it for.

A lot of people who otherwise love their work often become dismayed by factors such as pay, benefits, co-workers, working conditions, company politics, the boss, retirement, or perhaps employment uncertainty. They, too, would like things to be different. The best cure for this is more meaningful work and a busy, positively productive schedule leading to the achievement of a desired dream or goal. This helps take the focus off yourself and your challenges and puts it on helping others, which is the best way to get ahead in life. As the old adage goes, "It's 9-to-5 to survive, but after 5 to thrive."

Work is great medicine against boredom, depression, and mental fatigue, and the positive producer knows this. The more he or she works, the better his or her mood, health, and outlook on life are. The positive producer is so busy being productive that he or she has no time to become bored or depressed. After all, except in rare cases of chemical imbalance, depression can be something we bring on ourselves through our negative attitudes and behaviors. You can't be depressed when you're busy and positively productive.

Independent business ownership offers limitless opportunities. Sometimes it's something physical, such as sorting through prospect lists or files, sharing a product, service, or opportunity, cleaning out desk drawers, or making follow-up calls; sometimes it's something mental, such as brainstorming about ways to make a presentation more effective; and sometimes it's even something emotional, such as encouraging a prospect to have hope for his or her future, and to understand that he or she can get out of debt and build a better financial situation. Or it may simply be to extend the hand of friendship.

Speaking metaphorically, people who love to work and make a difference are usually the cream of society's crop—they typically rise to the top. But, as life insurance agents share with prospective clients, if you were to take a random group of 100 people and follow them from age 25 until 65, you would discover this: one person is wealthy, four are financially independent, five are still working to support themselves, 36 have already died, and the remaining 54 are essentially broke, often depending on relatives, the government, or charities to support them.

Was the wealthy person an employee for 40 years? Probably not. Did the four financially independent people get there simply by putting in 40 hours a week? Probably not. It's obvious that most people who become financially independent get there by working harder and smarter than average.

If you spend 21 percent of your week (40 hours) doing your work and 79 percent of your week (128 hours) using up the money you earned during 21 percent of the time, it stands to reason your expenditures are going to equal or exceed your income. The odds of making financial progress are almost four-to-one against you. And that's another strong motivation for positive producers to get into their own business.

So What About Money?

Now, you may be thinking that you don't have to be self-employed in order to find plenty of work to do. For sure, some employers allow people to work as many overtime hours as they wish. In fact, many companies *expect* their executives to go home each night with a briefcase full of reports, letters, calculations, and surveys to work on after dinner. And they don't even pay those often-harried workers anything extra.

As a person who has worked in public relations, I would be the last one to deny that some salaried or hourly wage jobs offer endless chances for work. The question is, however, why would you want to work endless hours without appropriate compensation? Why would you want to make someone else and his or her family prosperous when you could be doing something "after 5 to thrive"—and make *yourself* and *your family* prosperous?

True, there are people who answer to a religious, missionary, or volunteer calling. However, they have already decided upon a much different lifestyle and opted, in some cases from the start, not to become involved in the general business arena. Many of them rely on charitable contributions, industry, business, and the government to provide them with food and lodging, as well as other supplies, and even political protection.

For most of the rest of us, being an independent business owner is the key to financial security and personal progress. As a positive producer, I am not afraid to admit that I'm interested in earning money. That's why I worked beyond 5 p.m. to become a writer, professor, and consultant. The only limits on the amount of money I can earn from these activities are the opportunities I choose within these realms, and the limit I put on the time I work at them.

Let's get something straight right from the start: There is nothing evil or wrong about amassing a fortune by working hard and honestly. The concept of money being dirty or filthy is nonsense. A man or woman can be as evil on $1,000 or less a month as he or she can be on $100,000 or more a month and maybe more so. It is his or her *attitude* toward money and the way that person uses it—for good or evil purposes—not the amount of money itself which he or she earns or accumulates.

The Bible says, "The *love* of money is *a* root of evil." If a person lusts for money which he or she can hoard or stockpile or use for ill-conceived purposes, then this love of money surely can lead to evil doings. Money itself, however, is not evil. It's just a medium of exchange.

The integrity-based capitalism of the free enterprise system has helped participating nations become great. Honorably run free enterprise opportunities can truly enable people to flower, become the best they can be, and exceed the income limits imposed on wage earners. Free-enterprise nations, like the U.S., are likely to have a higher quality and greater number of schools, hospitals, social work agencies, retirement homes, colleges, universities, and other fine institutions than countries that have chosen not to utilize the free enterprise system. Many of these essential institutions are financed entirely, or in part, by private philanthropy or grants from businesses and foundations. For the majority of them, good people have put their honestly earned money to use for worthy purposes. As the Rev. Russell Herman Conwell said in 1893, "Money is power. Every good man and woman ought to strive for power, to do well with it when obtained. I say, get rich, get rich!" Many people worthy of emulation have lived by such a credo and, as a result, we have all benefited.

King Solomon knew that in every society "The rich ruleth over the poor, and the borrower is servant to the lender." As such, his advice was to be one of the rich or at least to associate with them. In this manner, a person has the opportunity to work with people or, preferably, be one of those who has the power to do a great deal of good for society. As he expressed it, "Seest thou a man diligent in his business? He shall stand before kings; he shall not stand before low men." For people who aspire to be wealthy, the sage advice is to associate with those who are where they desire to be, and duplicate their positive beliefs and actions.

British clergyman Rev. Sydney Smith wrote in 1807, "I have been very poor the greater part of my life and have borne it as well, I believe, as most people. But I can safely say that I have been happier for every guinea I have gained."

W. Somerset Maugham was a physician, novelist, short story author, and playwright. His works, including *Of Human Bondage* and *The Razor's Edge*, were extremely successful and popular during his lifetime of 91 years. He became very wealthy and, as he amassed more and more wealth, found that he was able to produce more writing of higher quality in a shorter time. In his autobiography, Maugham explained, "I found that money was like a sixth sense without which you could not make the most of the other five."

Money is something you can feel very good about. Contribute to society in an admirable, whole hearted way, and you can maximize your income potential as you go. When you love what you do and pour your heart and soul into it, you can't help but be rewarded monetarily. To Rev. Conwell, money was something used for doing good in the world. To Solomon, money was the key to the doors of power. To Rev. Smith, money was an element of personal happiness. To Maugham, money was a stimulus to creativity. Truly, money, as a tool used with integrity, can multiply our power for making a difference in our lives and the lives of others.

The Bible tells us that "the poor will always be with us," and we know that's true even in great prosperous nations. Regardless of the bounty around them, some people have a poverty mindset which serves to keep them in their state of destitution. This can be changed but only when, first of all, they latch onto a new, possibility-oriented attitude. Then they need to apply themselves to a worthy enterprise capable of lifting them to a new level of thinking and, therefore, a new level of income. By and large, free enterprisers who persevere have shown an uncanny resourcefulness for earning money—lots and lots of it.

The prosperous, free-enterprise oriented nations represent only a modest portion of the world's population, yet they have slightly more than half of the world's money and own more than three-quarters of the world's cars. We live in acres of diamonds. Food is plentiful for these nations and, in the eyes of the rest of the world, they do seem, as Solomon said, to "stand before kings."

But what is it that drives someone to become well-to-do? Dr. James A. Knight, M.D., a noted psychiatrist, poses the same question: "What does money mean to modern man? He earns, spends, and saves it. He dies for it; sometimes [unfortunately] kills for it. Why does man [apparently seem to be] in bondage to this inanimate thing, which he can use for both creative and destructive [purposes], that can make a prince a pauper and a bum a baron? One reads daily of charitable donations, of bank robberies, of inherited fortunes, occasionally of [money] found stuffed in an old mattress, and wonders about the personality traits, psychological problems, and attitudes that express themselves through the medium of money."

Dr. Knight later answers his own question about why people strive for money. He notes, "The original and basic aim is not for riches, but to enjoy power and respect among one's fellow men or within oneself. In our society, power and respect are mostly based on possession of money; this makes the need for power and respect a need for riches."

Although this is true, there is much more to it. For people to rise above the ordinary, gray mediocrity of the life of an average wage earner, they need more money. How can they achieve their dreams, big and small? How can they rid themselves of the burden of debt and the mundaneness of always barely getting by? How can they engross themselves in meaningful, enriching, expansive work that can reward them proportionately to the energies expended?

The answer is found in being a positive producer who is not tied to wage restrictions but, rather, empowered to fully engage in meaningful, financially fruitful activity. When such a scenario is bolstered by leveraging themselves in independent partnership, so to speak, with others who are of a like mind and heart, the positive-productivity experience is brought to a whole new level. Those fortunate enough to be a part of such an organization, networked with others, are truly blessed.

The positive producer has no modesty about expecting to gain substantial financial independence. He or she strives to earn large amounts of money because it provides security, leverage, opportunity, and luxury. As Dr. Knight expresses it, "Money serves as a medal of life's achievements" and aids as well in all that we set out to accomplish in life.

F. Scott Fitzgerald and Ernest Hemingway were together at a party given by some affluent people. Fitzgerald glanced around the room with all its fine furnishings and paintings and its guests all dressed in beautiful clothes and jewelry. "Ah, Hemingway," he mused, "the rich aren't like us. They're different." Hemingway, reportedly, swallowed his drink, put the glass back on a tray, and replied, "I know. They have more money."

Hemingway hit upon an element of bottom-line truth. Rich people *are* different, in that they travel more, buy more, own more, play more, control more, and have more say. But the only reason they do so is because "They have more money." They have the wherewithal to do these things. Their money gives them more options.

Old Tevye in the popular play *Fiddler on the Roof* sings a song titled, "If I Was a Rich Man." In it he dreams of how being wealthy would enable him to sit all day in the synagogue studying the ancient scriptures and gaining wisdom. Soon, he believes, people would seek his advice and ask his views on matters and then repeat his words to their friends.

How wonderful life would be…if only he could be a rich man.

Surely, like Tevye, we all have dreams of being wealthy. And that's fine. When we imagine greater things, we set our sights higher. Without this vision, there's little hope of having a much better life. But dreaming, alone, is not enough. It's the place we need to start, but it gets us nowhere by itself. Only positive productivity can move us toward obtaining our goal.

The positive producer is constantly aware of one basic rule of compensation: People get paid what the job's worth, not what they're worth. Society values various occupations more than others due to the level of education required, the responsibility required, or the revenue generation capability. But this doesn't mean any given occupation is more honorable than any other simply because it pays more. We all have a role to play and it's important for our well-being to love what we do.

However, if you want to earn more money, you do have some choices. First of all, you could simply do more of what you're already doing. But when you're on a salary, you won't earn more even if you work night and day. You could, of course, get a raise or a promotion, but then you'll probably have more responsibility and your employer will "own" you even more! You could also do what you're doing more effectively, get additional education and training in a field that commands more income, or leverage with others as an entrepreneur. But it's only this last choice that typically generates the most financial success.

To earn more income takes hard work and a genuine desire for becoming more successful. It calls for a commitment to continuing education in the form of reading, studying, listening, and watching; it demands extra time for planning and preparing; and it requires weeks, months, and years of personal and professional development. Those who consistently work hard and love what they do will become positive producers. And positive producers who build a strong independent business can have unimagined success and happiness.

The Rewards of Positive Productivity

Playing "Follow the Leader" instead of "Be the Leader" is an activity the general masses engage in every day. The positive producer, however, is a leader. He or she leads the way for others to follow. Work limitations like a set weekly salary and a standard 40-hour routine are unacceptable and, to say the least, impractical. The positive producer needs to have the freedom to work as long and as hard as he or she chooses.

One of the obvious primary rewards of positive producers who build a successful independent business is the ability to amass a substantial amount of money. Despite what some have said from time to time about the so-called evils of money, the truth is that obtaining wealth can be a very worthy and honorable goal. The financially independent person is not only someone who never becomes a burden to society, but he or she also is often someone who provides sustenance and help for the sick, uneducated, and aged people of the world. The positive producer gravitates toward independent business ownership because it offers limitless opportunities to work, produce, achieve, and succeed in life. As Jonas Salk, inventor of the polio vaccine said, "I feel that the greatest reward for doing is the opportunity to do more."

A great example of a positive producer is bicycle racer and cancer conquerer Lance Armstrong. In August of 2004, he won his sixth consecutive Tour de France (a grueling, three-week race around France)—an historic and unprecedented achievement. When interviewed on TV, he shared that he doesn't race bicycles for fame and fortune, but simply because he loves the sport! His love for the sport compelled him to work hard and, as a result, he has achieved great fame and fortune. He loves to work. And according to his mother, Linda, "Lance didn't get where he is today by sitting on the couch eating potato chips."

The other primary reward positive producers receive for building a successful business is what it causes them to become along the way. Overcoming the challenges inherit in becoming financially independent causes them to grow personally and become better people. By doing more, they create more relationships, have more experiences, and grow in wisdom. They learn more about others and themselves, as they grow and become the best they can be. As John Ruskin said, "The highest reward for a person's toil is not what they get for it but what they become by it."

"The highest reward for a person's toil is not what they get for it but what they become by it."

—John Ruskin

"Do you know who you are and the potential that lives inside of you, waiting to be released? We are all special, individualized beings capable of admirable accomplishments. And since we were born with the gifts of potential and desire, we need to discover and cultivate them. To know ourselves is to discover our desires and follow our dreams."

—Dennis E. Hensley

—3—

Know Yourself

*"People who have a plan for guiding
themselves and implement it discover, in the process,
who they really are."*
—Dennis E. Hensley—

In the opening chapter, I shared a bit about myself. And like you, I have experience and expertise in certain areas, while in others not so much or maybe none at all. Fortunately, it's not a matter of being gifted or talented that enables one to do well at something. It's simply a matter of desire, as author Bruce Garrabrandt explains so well in his book, *The Power of Having Desire.* You can do virtually anything you want to when you have a big enough desire!

The point here, however, is that I know *who* and *what* I am. Although I'm continually learning, disciplining myself, and challenging myself more and more, I am comfortable with my identity and I'm living the life I have chosen for myself—and loving it. And you can do the same. Establishing your own identity and then living comfortably with it is a worthy goal. The great minds of the ages have advised us to do just that. Socrates taught his students to "Know thyself," and Shakespeare wrote in *Hamlet*, "This above all: to thine own self be true."

But people have many sides to themselves, likes and dislikes, loves and hates, and noble and ignoble thoughts. Learning to know one's "self" can be a genuine challenge. Robert Louis Stevenson separated the dual natures of one man in his novel, *The Strange Case of Dr. Jekyll and Mr. Hyde*; it was horrifying. In *The Call of the Wild*, author Jack London allowed primitive animal instincts to arise in a domesticated dog, which caused him to become wild and savage. London noted in his journals that the dog was a metaphor for man, who also appears to be domesticated yet at times reverts to primitive savage behavior.

Even though writers sometimes provide us with an amplified, even exaggerated, look at a particular aspect of life, they nevertheless serve to make us aware of the potential (for good and bad) which mankind has. Writers then trust us to proceed in cautious, righteous, worthy, and useful ways. Quite often, unfortunately, that's more than some people are willing to give. But this doesn't have to be the case, as long as we have a viable plan for reaching our potential. When we implement it, we discover, in the process, who we really are. Then, with confidence, we can assert our identity. We can be people as purposeful as the leader of a larger organization; one who has a big dream and compassionately leads his or her people toward it by supporting them in accomplishing *their* dreams.

The bottom line is the same: to be a success, we need to know what success means to us and how to reach it by utilizing our full potential in an appropriate vehicle. We need to know ourselves and have a big dream. We need something more to strive for that calls us to action and stretches us to be better than we are.

An Honest Self-Evaluation

Now let's take a look at some attitudes and behaviors that people tend to respond to negatively.

The A to Z of Attitudes and Behaviors that People Often Respond to Negatively

Agressiveness	Jabbing	Stupidity
Browbeating	Kinkiness	Talkativeness
Cheating	Lateness	Unresponsiveness
Disrespectfulness	Morbidness	Vacillation
Egotism	Negativity	Whining
Flashiness	Overzealousness	Xenophobia*
Grumbling	Profanity	Yelling
Harassment	Quarreling	Zzzzz (Snoring)
Inconsiderateness	Reluctance	

* Fear or hatred of strangers or foreigners.

Which of these attitudes and behaviors, if any, do you exhibit? Are there any others? Now get a sheet of paper and list them.

Do you really know yourself? Perhaps an introduction is in order! Walk over to a full-length mirror and look at yourself. Stay there awhile. Look closely. Start at the top and examine yourself inch by inch. Have the nerve to let fantasies dissolve. If you see a receding hairline or a bald spot, don't mentally cover it by thinking back to the full head of hair you had when you were in high school. Then was then and now is now. This is how you look today. If you are bald, then recognize it. See yourself honestly as you really are.

Continue the analysis. Are you seeing bags under your eyes, an extra chin or two, a wrinkled neck, a bulging waistline, outdated clothes, or poor posture? If so, you are also seeing someone honest enough to face reality and courageous enough to make changes. I know what it's like. I've been there. Now it's time to...

Rank Your Goals and Strengths

Here are some personal goals as examples. Get a piece of paper and rank your personal goals according to their priorities:

( ) More time with family
( ) Better health and fitness
( ) More business adventures
( ) More leisure time
( ) Better social standing
( ) Getting out of debt

( ) More travel
( ) More overall accomplishments
( ) More personal influence
( ) More money
( ) Early retirement
( ) Financial Freedom

Now it's time to list and rank your business goals according to their priorities. Here are some examples:

( ) Greater productivity
( ) Higher income/bonuses
( ) Better reputation
( ) Increased leadership ability
( ) Improved client/associate relationships
( ) Continual expansion
( ) More enjoyable work
( ) Improved computer skills
( ) More education/knowledge

( ) Increased visibility
( ) Stronger ethics and standards
( ) More resiliency in handling the objections
( ) More professional recognition
( ) Increased and more effective presentations
( ) More financial reserves
( ) Better time/environment/activity management

List and rank your personal strengths related to business. Some of these may apply:

( ) Public speaking ability
( ) Recordkeeping
( ) People skills
( ) Products/services/opportunity promotional ability
( ) Neat and clean appearance
( ) Years of experience
( ) Knowledge/education

( ) Sense of humor
( ) Reputation
( ) Loyalty to business
( ) Product/service knowledge
( ) Ability to weather rejection
( ) Team spirit
( ) Writing ability
( ) Ability to organize

( ) Contacts   ( ) Time/environment/activity
( ) Capacity for careful planning   management skills
( ) Never-ceasing drive   ( ) Sufficient understanding of
( ) Track record   technology

Meeting a Different-Looking Person in the Mirror

One day, when I was 25 years old, I was shocked as I faced myself in the mirror. I awoke one morning only to discover that the entire left side of my face was completely distorted. One cheek was sagging; my lips were twisted; my left nostril was flat; my left eye was wide open because its eyelid was paralyzed and unable to blink; my forehead was wrinkled on the right side but paralyzed into smoothness on the left; even the left side of my tongue was numb. I was unable to talk clearly; I couldn't chew food or drink water without making a mess. It was maddening, not to mention frightening. The only thing I could imagine was that I had had a stroke of some sort. I went to the hospital right away.

"The good news is that you have not had a stroke," our family physician told me. "You have suffered a common nerve affliction known as Bell's Palsy. The bad news is that it's going to keep your face malformed like that for several weeks and even months. And, most likely, you will never recover completely."

He was right. After about three months, I could speak and eat fairly normally again, and the numbness left my tongue, lips, and cheek. Once again, I could wrinkle my forehead and blink my eyelids.

But, despite these improvements, there were also signs of permanent damage. My smile was lopsided; I could not form my lips into a circle for whistling; breathing out of the left side of my nose was still difficult; and, worst of all, my left eyelid was permanently drooped at about half-mast.

55

The whole situation seemed incredible. I would look into the mirror and not recognize the face looking back at me. How could this have happened? I had earned half a dozen combat medals during the war in Vietnam and had come home virtually without a scratch. However, now, at age 25, in the peacefulness of my own home, I had suffered irrepairable bodily damage. Talk about grim irony.

For a while I became a recluse. I stayed home, avoided old friends, and declined invitations. When I did have to go out, I wore a patch over my left eye, pulled my hat down low, and raised the collar of my coat.

The adjustment to the new me—the *real* physical me, the me I was going to be living with for the rest of my life—came slowly at first. I had a negative opinion of myself; I saw only my outward appearance; and I was displeased and depressed.

Fortunately, however, my friends also saw the inner me. When I quit calling them, they came in search of me. When an old friend would see me again for the first time, he or she would look surprised, but certainly not disgusted or annoyed at my appearance. After some standard questions such as "Does it hurt?" or a comment like "My aunt had something like that once," our conversations would move in directions they normally would have, just as if I had never suffered the paralysis! My new look was affecting no one else as much as it was affecting me, so having the right attitude was more important than ever. As a result, I came up with...

The Seven Maxims of a Right Attitude

1. Real winners achieve their success through honest hard work.

2. My attitude of strength *is* my strength.

3. I enjoy my work because_____.

4. There is no such thing as luck; there is only hard work which prepares me for forthcoming opportunities.

5. I am admired because I have an I-do-what-I-say reputation and a work record of positive productivity.

6. I am too busy focusing on helping others and achieving my goals to be petty about anything.

7. I keep an open mind because I am always eager to learn more and, thereby, advance myself to the next level.

As my friends kindly and unconditionally supported me, I began to realize I had been suffering from shock. It wasn't that I wasn't strong enough to accept my changed appearance nor was it a case of my being too vain, proud, scared, or naive to deal with my new circumstances. It was simply that I had been given no time to prepare myself for this extremely new and challenging situation. I had been caught completely unaware, fully off-guard. And I had reacted instinctively rather than responding thoughtfully. I had dreaded the worst rather than planned for the best. I had let my attitude control me instead of me controlling it!

After having come to grips with the fact that the facial paralysis had not changed the internal me, I decided to tackle the challenge of my disorder with the same vigor and intensity I had always tackled every other challenge in my life. I began by going back to the mirror.

When I looked at myself this time, I painted no imaginative cosmetic pictures of what I once had been or what I hoped I would somehow miraculously become again. I looked at myself truthfully, smiled the best lopsided smile I could muster, and said, "Okay, so you'll never be a model or a movie star. Hardly the end of the world, right? Right! So, let's take it from here."

From that point on, I grew stronger every day. I grew physically stronger by using a special vibrator to stimulate my facial muscles, by practicing to enunciate words distinctly (despite the lip and nasal challenges) and by holding my head high for a change. I grew spiritually stronger by spending extra time in prayer. And I grew mentally stronger by enrolling in a Ph.D. program in English, and expanding my freelance writing career.

Now, more than 30 years later, I am so accustomed to the new me, it surprises me as much as anyone when people at a class reunion ask, "Hey, what happened to your eye?"

Confronting and learning to accept the reality of my new appearance gave me renewed confidence, strength, direction, and purpose. Truth be told, I have to admit that the attack of Bell's Palsy was one of the most beneficial setbacks I have ever encountered—as paradoxical as that may seem.

Straight Talk—*Use It to Move Ahead*

It's a proven fact that people who speak well are likely to advance more rapidly in their careers or businesses. Here are some tips for improving your vocal appeal:

- Keep your language unoffensive—avoid profanity and slang.

- Increase your vocabulary regularly.

- Speak in complete sentences.

- Pronounce words clearly and correctly.

- Develop a consistently pleasing tonal quality.

• Be clear and concise in your communications.

The Emotional You

We need to be alert to how we may be unskillfully reacting to any given situation so we can change, if necessary, to a more healthy response. Otherwise, we can let the occurrences we face in life put us on an emotional roller coaster. In order to become more stable and more in control of our attitudes and lives, we need to recognize the internal and external factors which cause us to generate certain emotional responses. Ask yourself why you responded in an inappropriate way. Sit quietly and consider the following ten questions, and write down as many responses as you can think of to each one. Afterward, ask yourself, "Now that I've recognized these emotional responses, what can I do to make use of them or control them?" List those responses too.

1. What sort of things do I get angry about?

2. When did I last enjoy a hearty laugh?

3. Am I ashamed to cry? Why?

4. When frustrated or in a hurry, do I still communicate clearly?

5. What situations do I find stressful?

6. Am I generally optimistic or pessimistic?

7. What triggers me to act with impatience?

8. Do I have any nervous habits such as nail biting?

9. In what circumstances do I feel secure or insecure? Why?

10. When was the last time I had insomnia? What caused it?

Consider this: I needed to lose myself in continuous mental concentration for a positive aim, so I wouldn't just dwell on my misfortune. Therefore, I went back to college. Today I am a doctor of English. My need to spend many hours in speech readjustment and oratory practice helped me to develop good public speaking skills. As a result, I've been speaking for years at conventions, universities, conferences, and business meetings, as well as teaching a full load of classes at Taylor University each semester.

I could cite numerous other benefits that came out of such an experience, but getting to know yourself—no matter how challenging that may be—is one of the most wonderful benefits in life.

Turning Negatives into Positives

Be open to the possibility of discovering negative factors about yourself. Even harsh reality is good reality when you use it to make a positive shift. Did you know that in the Japanese language the character drawing that represents the word setback is the very same symbol for the word opportunity? It's true. And it's true in life too. It's all in how you look at things. Is that upset apple cart a giant mess or is it the discovery of applesauce? Is that singed piece of glass a ruined window or is it the invention of sunglasses? It's all in how you perceive things that show up in your life.

I have two good friends, Don and Sandy, who look for positive things in everything that happens to them in their married life. When a big sinkhole appeared in their lawn one day, their neighbors said it was too bad. However, Don disagreed. It gave him a great idea to get rid of excess water buildup on his land! When Sandy almost burned down their house by forgetting to turn off the stove while cooking hamburger, she made the decision to prepare cooked foods at the ice cream business she and Don owned. They bought the needed equipment, expanded their line of food offerings, and doubled their business within two seasons. This happy couple looks for the opportunities presented by all setbacks.

Becoming Self-Motivated

"A motive is an urge within an individual that incites him or her to action. It is the hope or other force that moves the individual to produce specific results."

—W. Clement Stone

Here are seven key elements for turning inaction into action:

1. Become aware of what your true desires are.

2. Get excited about and determined to obtain those desires.

3. Develop discipline in pursuing them step by step.

4. Upraise your enthusiasm and optimism about each of your achievements along the way. Show appreciation for any help you received.

5. See challenges as opportunities, and be open to the possibilities they present.

6. Increase your confidence by becoming knowledgeable in your field.

7. Focus on becoming the successful person you've dreamed of becoming.

Make a list of what you need to do or do more of to spark yourself into action. Keep it in front of you.

Re-Conceptualization

When it comes to perceiving our own potential, most of us would do well to take a lesson from marketing experts.

Whenever a marketing consultant is brought in to build sales for a waning business, the first thing he or she does is to re-conceptualize the business. The consultant may not suggest changing the business itself, but rather the way customers and other people perceive it.

Now let's take a look at how you typically appear to others. What do you need to do this week to make some changes? See the following checklist and answer each question yes or no. Write down the changes you need to make and the actions you need to take.

Personal Appearance Checklist

Question	Yes	No	Changes Needed/Next Action Step
Is my hair washed, styled, curled (as appropriate), and brushed/combed?			
Are my eyeglasses at least fairly contemporary in style?			
Are my teeth as clean and white and in as good repair as possible?			
Is my breath unoffensive?			
Do I often smile?			
Is my weight what it needs to be?			
Am I clean and shaven?			
Are my clothes clean, pressed, and reasonably up to date?			
Are my shoes in repair and cleaned/shined?			
Is my posture straight?			
Are my fingernails clean, trimmed, and polished (if appropriate)?			
Do I have good hygiene?			
Is my jewelry clean and nice-looking but not gaudy or pretentious?			
Is my briefcase professional looking and well-kept inside and out?			
Do I always carry professional looking business cards?			

Yes! Appearances can make all the difference. For example, a town may have seven used car dealers, but only one "pre-owned vehicle" dealer...and it's the latter that's more likely to draw new customers. A city may have 20 optical stores, but only one "eye care boutique"...and it's the latter that will get the lion's share of the youth-oriented business. The businesses themselves may be basically the same; it's just that they have re-conceptualized how they present themselves and have capitalized on it.

You can do the same thing! Can you re-conceptualize "old age" as "vintage maturity"? Can you re-conceptualize "past your prime" as "at the summit"? Can you change "youthful inexperience" to "open-minded enthusiasm"? Can "undereducated" become "always learning more"? Can "greenhorn" become "latest new protégé"?

Of course! Of course! Of course!

It's all a matter of going to that mirror and taking a fresh look at yourself. See the you the world sees, discover your strengths and capitalize on them, and admit your weaknesses and overcome them. If you don't like the quality of the work you are doing now, start doing better. If you don't like the look you are projecting now, re-conceptualize yourself and project a new look. This is all part of being a positive producer.

Throughout this chapter you have noticed questionnaires, guides, and idea lists, and it was suggested that you respond to these items—*in writing*. Keep those responses in a special file and review them each month. See how you are changing, maturing, and growing. Note the progress of any re-conceptualization goals you have set for yourself. Completely retest yourself every six months to discover any changes in your needs, opinions, and goals. In short, keep in touch with yourself. This is a prerequisite to associating with and helping others most effectively with your product, service, or opportunity. If you seem to be stuck in your ability to be a growing positive producer, ask for help from people who are where you want to be.

The Hidden You

Despite the fact you may tell folks you were "born to eat caviar," you may, in truth, be more like "the salt of the earth." Either way, you can be a happy, joyful, positive person. Answer the following ten questions. Do any patterns emerge? If so, what do they reveal about who you really are, what you really want, and how you need to proceed to get it?

1. If I had all my time and money challenges handled, what would I do? What hidden desires may I be ignoring? Who would I spend more time with? Where would I go? What would I buy?

2. What is my next simple action step to move forward to achieve my goals/dreams?

3. How happy am I *really* about what I am doing?

4. How might I be holding myself back and why? What excuses might I be making?

5. How can I give myself a sense of urgency to get moving? Do I realize that I am not going to live forever and that any procrastinating I may be doing is delaying my achievement of the better life I yearn for?

6. What tapes/CDs/videos/DVDs can help me?

7. What positive, uplifting, growth-encouraging books do I need to read to become a more positive producer?

8. What helpful skills and attitudes do I already have? Which ones do I need to develop?

9. What training sessions, seminars, conventions, opportunity meetings, product fairs, and other motivational, continuing education-type meetings and get-togethers do I need to attend?

10. Am I always taking notes, asking questions, and exhibiting an open, teachable attitude? If not, what do I need to do to get started?

Do you know who you are, and do you realize the potential that lies inside of you just waiting to be released? It's an awesome question to consider. We are all special, individualized beings, capable of admirable accomplishments. And since we were born with the gifts of potential and desire, would it not follow that we need to discover them within ourselves and cultivate them? To *know yourself* is to follow your dreams and discover your capabilities as you do.

"When you start devoting more of your prime time to your priorities, you'll discover that you won't have time to do most of the time-filler things you used to do. A lot of them were simply avoidance items—some of which others may do or, perhaps, don't need to be done at all."

—Dennis E. Hensley

–4–

Lead Yourself and Empower Others— Work Smarter, Not Just Harder

"Every time you teach someone else how to do something new and they follow your lead, you free yourself from that activity and increase your productivity."
—Dennis E. Hensley—

There's an old joke which relates well to the misconceptions many people have about the best use of their time, so they can wisely lead themselves. One day a man was driving by an apple orchard when he happened to see a farmer lifting his pigs, one at a time, up to the tree branches so that they could eat the apples. The man stopped his car, got out, and approached the farmer. "Excuse me," he said, "but isn't that an awfully time-consuming practice?" The farmer looked at the man, shrugged his shoulders, and said, "So? What's time to a pig?"

Whereas the absurdity of the farmer's situation in this story is obvious, situations which are equally as absurd, yet not nearly as obvious, exist in countless businesses, shops, and offices today. It behooves the positive producer to examine his or her time/activity management habits. The greatest desire in the world to be a positive producer is of no value if a person's work is simply wheelspinning busyness rather than forward-moving productivity. The wheelspinning is synonymous with many typical societal experiences which lead to a life of monotony and frustration—basic survival at best.

This chapter will help you gauge how well you are now using your time. You will learn about some basic steps you can take to become more productive with the time you have. Let's begin by determining how you are currently leading yourself and empowering others.

Leading Yourself and Empowering Others— *How Do You Rate?*

Circle either "Yes" or "No" to the following questions: Do you...

1. Start the day or evening by thinking through, and writing down what you need to do to further yourself toward achieving your dreams and goals? **Yes No**

2. Think through a task before starting it. **Yes No**

3. Complete tasks to the best of your ability rather than leaving them partially done? **Yes No**

4. Do the most important tasks first even if they are more challenging? **Yes No**

5. Inspire and encourage people to pursue their dreams, accomplish their goals, and achieve their own success?

    Yes No

6. Empower people to keep stretching beyond what they've done before?   **Yes No**

7. Say no if someone asks you to do something that would interfere with your priorities?   **Yes No**

8. Do you use a machine or computer when it's more effective than doing things manually?   **Yes No**

9. Leverage well by inspiring and empowering others to do things themselves rather than trying to do everything yourself?   **Yes No**

10. Regularly venture out and do new things toward achieving your dreams and goals?   **Yes No**

11. Have an open mind about doing things differently rather than being held back by your old ways of thinking?   **Yes No**

12. Redirect yourself if you go off on a tangent and get off track, for example, by starting projects you have little interest in or know you probably will not finish?   **Yes No**

13. Teach others, first of all, how to accomplish easy short-term goals to help them build their confidence?

    Yes No

14. Operate by preventive planning instead of waiting until a crisis occurs?   **Yes No**

15. Put people first by handling associates' and clients' concerns as soon as reasonably possible?   **Yes No**

16. Refuse to socialize either in person or on the phone with friends or family during a time when you need to be productive? **Yes No**

17. Do you avoid being distracted during times of potential positive productivity by such things as newspapers, magazines, TV, friends, hobby activities, sports, playing on the computer, low priority voicemail or email, mail, and other nonproductive activities? **Yes No**

18. Group errands efficiently together rather than making several individual trip? **Yes No**

19. Ask for help from your leader or mentor about ways to become more of a positive producer? **Yes No**

20. Always focus on the best use of every minute of every day and help others to do the same? **Yes No**

To rate yourself, count the number of Yes and No answers. If you answered No more than Yes, you are wasting time and not being as productive and effective in empowering others as you could be. If you have 5-10 No answers, then you need to improve your ability to lead yourself and others. If you answered No to more than 15 questions, you also need to reassess your priorities and increase your focus on them.

Conditioned Responses

To begin with, while it's true that everyone is given the same number of hours each day, days each week, weeks each month, and so on, it is also true that no two people feel the same about time. Clocks, schedules, deadlines, calendars, and history books evoke different emotions from different people.

Most of these emotions are conditioned responses, formed in the conscious and subconscious minds of individuals through various experiences and how they perceived those experiences. A good experience repeated frequently will most likely develop into a good attitude. A bad experience, repeated frequently, on the other hand, may elicit a bad attitude, especially if the person has yet to learn that there is always something good to be gleaned out of a so-called bad experience. This was proven recently when a major company switched paydays from Fridays to Mondays. The employees quit saying, "Thank goodness it's Friday" as much as they used to. Furthermore, the rate of absenteeism on Mondays was cut by more than 30 percent. People arrived at work smiling instead of frowning, moaning, and groaning.

Knowing this, have you ever endeavored to analyze why you feel as you do about matters related to time? Give yourself a simple task analysis test. What emotions do you feel when you hear each of these words: *late...work...pressure...deadline...interruptions...stall... procrastination...race...waiting...stopwatch...timeclock ...start...stop...schedule?*

You'll probably find that your emotional responses to time-related words vary greatly. That's typical, even among those who have similar jobs or businesses, schedules, and social lives.

To the person who hates going to work, as two out of three people do, the sound of an alarm clock is dreadful. It announces the start of another boring or stressful day of putting time in for the paycheck. Whereas to another person, perhaps an enthusiastic business owner, the alarm signals an exciting chance to get into the day's activities—to be as positively productive and have as much fun as possible. To another person who is service-oriented, both to associates and clients, frequent interruptions are reminders of the fact that he or she is vitally important to every business activity. To those with a negative attitude, frequent interruptions are aggravating work-stopping frustrations, which are not appreciated and maybe even resented. That's sad. After all, we are here to serve—that's how we earn our income.

Observe your own emotional responses to time and situations. If you identify negative feelings (which stem from negative thoughts) that cause you to react in a negative way, you can work to reshape them to more positive thinking, feelings, and behavior. When you identify positive feelings, you can feel confident about them and the responsibilities you have, as a positive producer, to invest your energies wisely. You can call these feelings back, by remembering what triggered them. You can repeat them at will to more directly motivate yourself and empower others. Control over attitude is one of the secrets of winners.

Maximize the (ROI) Return on Investment of Your Time and Energy—*Be Productive, Not Just Busy*

The most common negative feeling about time is a sense of being *busy* but not particularly *productive*. Studies have shown that no matter what business a person may be in, he or she is subject to the "80/20 rule." Invariably, 20 percent of what a person does yields 80 percent of his or her progress; while 80 percent of a person's time is usually spent on busywork, which produces only 20 percent of that person's total accomplishments.

The only real way to get more leverage over the 80/20 rule is to establish priorities, and then devote time to each item according to its ranking. For example, don't be chatting aimlessly with your neighbor about the latest negative news, when you could be calling and building a relationship with a potential prospect or associate; don't let yourself be stuck talking purposelessly with people you know at an event where you could be meeting new people and building your career or business. Stay on each task until it is either completed or moved along as far as you can push it for that day or evening. Don't fill your time with numerous "go-for" jobs, which, perhaps, someone else could do, when you need to be *investing* your time to fulfill a major objective.

Take the highest priority task first each day. Begin as early as possible in the day or evening, working on your top-priority items. You can accomplish two things by doing this: First, you guarantee that real progress will be made; and second, you remain more in control of what you accomplish, even if interruptions arise later (because your priority items have already been completed or have been well-advanced). After you handle an interruption, which may mean just writing yourself a reminder note to do something later, or handle it right away if it's going to take two minutes or less, get back on track with your priorities. You can use a "Focusing on Priorities" chart to learn how to set up your daily tasks by priority rankings.

Focusing on Priorities

Ranking	Item	Goal or Deadline	Next Action	Who Else Could Do It?
Priority				
Especially Important				
Important				
Routine/Maint.				
Unessential				

Use your prime time on your priorities, doing one at a time and staying with it until it is completed (or moved along as far as you can take it at that time). The above chart will help you identify and focus on the tasks which really merit and require your priority attention to accomplish what you truly need and want to achieve.

When you start devoting more of your prime time to your priorities, you'll discover that you won't have time to do many of the time-filler things you used to do. You're likely to find a lot of them were simply avoidance items—some of which others may even do better or, perhaps, don't need to be done at all.

Parkinson's law says that, "Work expands to fill the time available for its completion." But positive producers don't buy into it. In fact, they have a sense of urgency about accomplishing things and consistently strive to do *more* in *less* time!

Take a few minutes to list the things you are in the habit of doing but which are not really related to your dreams, goals, and objectives. For instance, are you alphabetizing and filing prospects' names instead of just calling them? Are you hanging around people who are trying to discourage you from pursuing your dreams or associating with others who are going somewhere? Are you still handling responsibilities that others could easily do instead? Are you just socializing with your associates instead of taking an interest in them and encouraging them to grow? If you said yes to these or similar questions, begin immediately to do whatever it takes to drop those time-wasting practices. You'll be amazed at how this will free you up to accomplish more!

Leverage Your Time—*Teach and Empower Others to Do What You've Been Doing*

One of the best ways to eliminate what would be just time-filler activities is to give them to someone else who could better benefit by doing them. The more you empower others, while leveraging your time, the more freedom you'll have. This is essential for those who want to lead, particularly in business. The chart on the next page can help you brainstorm ways to empower others. Before you begin, ask yourself these four questions about what you're doing in your career or business:

1. Is what I'm doing part of the system of success I've been taught for the business or industry that I'm in? (Am I empowering or distracting people with my example?)

2. Is it duplicatable? (Can my associates easily do what I'm doing?)

3. What do I need to do next to teach my associates how to move on more effectively to achieve their dreams and goals?

4. Is there someone more knowledgeable and experienced than I am who could help me better leverage myself?

Are you doing work personally or in your career or business that could be better done by others? Every time you teach and empower someone else to do a task, you can free yourself from that activity and provide more time for what you, personally, want or need to be doing.

Think of three routine tasks you now do regularly which you could have someone else do. See the following example for ideas:

Task	Frequency
Mow the lawn	Once a week
Babysitting	When we do evening/weekend business activites
Clean house/apartment	Bi-weekly

Now, prepare a specific plan for having someone else do those tasks:

Task	Delegated To	In This Way
Mow the lawn	Son/Daughter	Assign one of the kids or hire Joe, the teacher who mows lawns part-time, for a very reasonable price.
Babysitting	Mom, Sister, or Neighbor	A week before, call Mom, Ann, or Jen to babysit.
Clean house/apartment	Son/Daughter	Create a chart of the kids' responsibilities and monitor them.

In leading ourselves and empowering others, we need to think about the return on the hour invested. For every hour devoted to our careers or businesses and the quality of our lives, we need to ask ourselves how much return (income, profits, enjoyment, or recognition) we are receiving. That's when we become more conscious of how well we are investing our time. The following activities can help you do that.

Gauge Your Time

Do you know specifically what you do during the hours of your day and the days of your week? To find out, keep an hourly log of all of your activities—both business and personal. After a week of doing so, simply add up the hours you spent doing each activity. This will help you determine whether you are using time wisely or simply squandering it.

Activity	Time Unplanned	Time Planned
Amusement		
Civic		
Family		
Phone Calling		
Continuing Education		
Eating		
Office Work		
Prospecting		
Religious		
Sleeping		
Studying		
Watching TV		
Surfing the Web		
Thinking & Planning		
Traveling		
Waiting		
Other		

The Paper Mill

A simple way to maximize the return on your investment of time is to develop concentrated tunnel vision. Whenever you need to work through a business challenge, clear your work area of everything which does not specifically relate to it. This will eliminate distracting clutter and also, as mentioned previously, allow you to focus on the top priority item until the task is completed. As each task is finished, clear off that task's materials and replace them with the next task's materials (lists, folders, books, maps, files, etc.). Proceed, then, as before, and do your best to maintain control, at all times, over the paper that comes into your personal and business life. Have "inboxes" for unaddressed items—one for business and one for personal.

Paper shuffling has long been recognized as a great time-wasting process. The computer has helped to some degree with this but, in reality, has actually created more paper! And most people hang onto notes, memos, and reports as though they were running a national archive. They pile them up virtually forever in view. That sort of extreme caution can be costly both in time and money, and is generally needless. If you need to, quickly file these items out of sight but easily accessible.

Some people receive hundreds of nonessential e-mails each week because they have their names on forward-to lists. Getting off these lists, as appropriate to your goals, can save valuable, productive time. Here are some other time-saving ideas:

1. *Pitch it whenever possible.* If someone else, like your spouse, for example, has filed a copy of the information you're holding, you can probably destroy

or delete your copy. If it's not a legal document, permanent historical record, or vital resource reference, discard or delete whatever record you have. Use your business website in lieu of having many miscellaneous catalogs which can be distracting. Keep only current catalogs pertinent to your business or objective. Toss all junk mail into the wastebasket as soon as it arrives. Go through your files once a year and toss out what you don't need.

2. *Seek condensed material.* Don't request data, statistics, or reports unless they are vital; if they truly are needed, get a digest version or a pertinent excerpt from a longer report. Rather than have a paper report, use on-line files as much as you can.

3. *Handle paper just once.* Respond to memos or letters when they come in, even if it's not a priority, if you can do so in two minutes or less. Read reports, e-mails, pamphlets, or brochures in one sitting, scanning for information pertinent to what you're doing, and highlighting what's important to you.

4. *Rely on short responses.* Never send a letter if you can jot a note on a postcard or do an e-mail. Never write a report if you can do a quick memo or e-mail. Be concise, yet friendly and kind.

5. *Purge your files.* Review your total filing system every 12 months, and discard as much paper as possible. Cancel any suspended-operations files or redesignate to a secondary, less accessible file system. Eliminate seldom-used reference files, as long as you can easily get the information elsewhere. Save time and space by keeping a fast-grab file on your desk,

or in your computer document file, containing frequently called phone numbers, deadline reminders, and lists of projects to brainstorm about before tackling. Keep your e-mail address book honed to key people.

Each day, do all you can to fill the wastebasket (both paper and computer) rather than endlessly stuffing your files with useless information because you may not know what to do with it.

Stop the Stopping Habit

Benjamin Franklin said, "The two things I hate most about each day's activities are going to bed and getting out of bed." In his own homespun way, Franklin had explained what time and motion experts now refer to as the power of inertia.

In essence, the power of inertia makes us want to continue to do what we are currently doing. If we are resting, we tend to stay sitting or in bed. If we are working, we tend to remain working. Knowing this helps us understand why procrastination is so common. Unless we force ourselves to take the first action step toward getting started on a task and overcome inertia, it remains easier to keep doing time-filling maintenance and avoidance activities. Procrastination is the worst habit a potential positive producer can develop. Many dreams and goals go by the wayside simply because people have perpetual, success-stealing, life-draining procrastination habits.

Procrastination is a lot like lying. Some people say they'll do something but don't follow through. Procrastinating even a little leads to a bad habit which, before long, can lead to serious trouble. And even though all activities are not equally enjoyable, and getting started can often be challenging, there are ways to overcome this.

If a task seems overwhelming, remember what Henry Ford said about no job being too difficult as long as it is broken down into several smaller jobs. That bit of wisdom, incidentally, helped me learn to write books. After many years of working as a newspaper columnist and magazine feature writer, I was asked to write a very long and detailed book about the life and writings of American author Jack London.

Having never written anything longer than 3,000 words, writing a book seemed like it would be a daunting task. Sensing the apprehension, my publisher said, "Don't think of it as 325-page book. Think of the 15 chapters as 15 individual feature articles on a related topic. When the 15 articles in the series are done, we'll assemble them as a collection and that will become the book." With this new perspective, I wrote the 15 articles and a year or so later my first book was published.

You can follow the same approach. If ever a task seems immense, focus only on the first action step; complete that step and then move on to the next. You will be encouraged as you finish something each day. It will give you the confidence and motivation you'll need to beat procrastination.

Timely Advice

As I noted earlier, this chapter cannot pretend to offer you a thorough study of all aspects of leading yourself and empowering others. For that, I recommend that you ask your leader or mentor about what book and tape or CD he or she might recommend. Read or listen to it, take notes, and put into action what you learn. Don't be one of those people who say, "I'm going to spend some time studying leading myself and empowering others…just as soon as I can get around to it!"

In the meantime, here's an overview—an A-to-Z primer—of ways to work more effectively and become more conscious of how you lead yourself and empower others.

A Instead of punishing yourself for wasting time, give yourself rewards each time you lead yourself wisely, and stay focused on your professional and personal priorities. Reinforce yourself in a positive way.

B. Learn to say no without feeling guilty. If you are asked to do something and you know you have other priorities which preclude your doing it to the best of your ability, just say no. You can do more damage by doing a halfway job of something than you can by kindly refusing to get involved in the first place.

C. Plan your work activities and then persistently and actively work your plan.

D. Never consider defeat. Concentrate on your strengths, and fine-tune any areas that could threaten to impede your progress.

E. Link tasks together. Whenever possible, do two things at once. For example, stuff envelopes while talking on the phone, or listen to a continuing education tape or CD while doing your morning and evening bathroom routines, or while taking a walk.

F. Do away with the open-door policy as much as possible. You need tranquility and uninterrupted time whenever you are concentrating. Constant interruptions are productivity stealers.

G. Have fewer and shorter meetings. Prepare a specific agenda ahead of time and stick to it. Keep attendees on track and focused.

H. Plan your 24-hour segments by filling in a daily schedule and planner each night before bed (see sample at the end of the chapter). Stick to your plan each day. Allow for interruptions, deal with them, and get right back to your priorities as soon as they are dealt with.

I. Set goals and strive to reach them by specific target dates. If you need to, reset the goals until you achieve them.

J. Courageously speak up if someone else's slow work is delaying the completion of one of your tasks. Communicate your concerns to the appropriate person in a frank, friendly, fair, and firm way.

K. Stay radiantly healthy. Take vitamins and food supplements, exercise regularly, eat nutritious foods, keep your weight within the recommended range, and get adequate sleep and regular medical checkups. Time spent sick is wasted.

L. Return calls just before noon or just before 5:00 p.m. and whenever you are in a bit of a hurry. This will help to keep you focused on the reason for the call and prevent the other person from rambling.

M. Use commuting time to listen to tapes or CDs that can help you to get motivated or teach you something. Instead of getting into the car each morning and evening and listening to the radio, play a tape or CD that teaches you how to build your business or client base, handle various challenges, and personally develop and maintain a great attitude.

N. Set up your briefcase so it contains something positive to read, and something to write with and on. When waiting for a plane or train, stuck in traffic, or sitting in a waiting room, you'll be able to invest that time wisely.

O. Instead of long coffee breaks, take five-minute work pauses. This will refresh you, but not give you time to lose your momentum.

P. Learn from your mistakes and don't repeat them.

Q. Remember Parkinson's Law: "Work expands to fill the time available for its completion." If you give yourself three days to complete a task, you'll take at least three days; if you give yourself three hours, you'll take at least three hours. Make your goal times optimistic and challenging. Motivate yourself to do more in less time.

R. Always anticipate and welcome change as an opportunity to grow. Prepare for it and adapt quickly when it comes, including embracing technological innovations.

S. As affordable and appropriate, use machines which will save you time: cell phones, calculators, computers, pagers, VCRs, CD and DVD players, and Palm Pilots.

T. Remember this rule of decision-making: "Learn to make a decision—lead, follow, or get out of the way!"

U. Eat light lunches and suppers. Heavy midday and evening meals make you sluggish.

V. Carry two books with you at all times: a positive one to read when you are caught with extra time, and one with blank pages (could be your planner) so that you can write down any good ideas which come into your mind.

W. Arrange your work area so that you can reach your telephone, wastebasket, in/out trays, computer, file cabinet, intercom, and bulletin board without having to stand.

X. Use "white noise" (e.g, the hum of a dehumidifier, pleasant instrumental music without lyrics) to override external distracting noises.

Y. Short naps provide bonus energy for the body. Napoleon Bonaparte, Jules Verne, Thomas Edison, Bill Gates, and Colin Powell all use or used 15-minute naps to revitalize themselves. Lay your head down, clear your mind of all thoughts, breathe evenly, and doze off for a few moments.

Z. Build some slack time into your daily schedule and planner (e.g., one open appointment hour or a shorter lunch-hour break) so that unforeseen interruptions can be more easily handled.

Daily Schedule and Planner

Today's Date: _____

This Week's Goal: _____

This Month's Goal:_____

This Year's Main Priority: _____

To be an effective positive producer, you need to invest your time and energy wisely by consciously leading yourself and empowering others to do the same. Continually ask yourself, "How much return on my investment of this hour am I getting right now? Am I doing the highest priority task in the best way possible? Am I doing whatever it takes?"

My Life Priorities:	Today's Priority Action Step:		Typing to Do:
	Ongoing Tasks:		
Emails or Letters to Write:	**Phone Calls to Make:**	**Appointments and Other Scheduled Business Activities:**	**Miscellaneous:**

"To be an effective positive producer, you need to invest your time and energy wisely by consciously leading yourself and empowering others to do the same. Continually ask yourself, 'How much return on my investment of this hour am I getting right now? Am I doing the highest priority task in the best way possible? Am I doing whatever it takes?'"

—Dennis E. Hensley

"If you're excited about building a business, don't let anyone—especially yourself— slow you down. The reason you became an independent business owner, to begin with, was because you have a <u>dream</u> or <u>goal</u> and you like the challenge and excitement of the work. Right? Stay psyched-up. It'll keep the stress away and keep you energized through the challenges."

—Dennis Hensley

_5_

Special Opportunities for Growth Available to Positive Producers

"Few people during their lifetime come anywhere near exhausting the resources within them. There are deep wells of strength that are never used."
—Richard E. Bryd—

There are many reasons for and benefits to be potentially gained by becoming a positive producer, including: security, altruism, independence, a more enjoyable lifestyle, financial freedom, recognition, flexibility of schedule, admirable performance, greater influence, discovery and development of better health, personal growth, and more.

Although the positive producer will, with dedicated persistence, build a better life and career or business, it won't happen overnight. Nor will it eliminate all of life's challenges. Death and taxes, for example, are here to stay. But unlike those two certainties, most situations can be overcome and, in the process, will lead to greater success and happiness.

Let's see how positive producers overcome and deal with stress.

Challenges Are Opportunities for Growth—*Welcome Them with Open Arms*

The first thing I learned after leaving the teaching profession to become a P.R. (public relations) executive was that my chief function each day would be to serve as a troubleshooter. Whenever there were internal cooperation challenges among employees, the P.R. people were called in as referees. When there was a poor public perception of the organization, the P.R. people were told to correct it. When there was a lack of visibility, a falling away of clientele, a communication foul-up between departments, or even a poor menu selection in the cafeteria, the P.R. department usually got the first call.

For a while, I was mystified by all the calls. "*Why me?*" I wondered. When the grounds look shabby around our buildings, why not call the maintenance department? When the daily mail distribution is running late, why not call the control dispatcher? Why did everyone automatically assume that P.R. needed to be called to resolve every challenge?

After being on the job a few months, the answer became obvious. P.R. workers seemed to have a reputation for putting out fires, abating storms, and calming troubled waters. The metaphors might have varied, but the substance was the same: P.R. people were seen as *professional challenge-overcomers*.

As you become more of a positive producer, you are going to gain the reputation of someone who gets things done—and done right! More and more people are going to turn to you as a leader. As you assist them in overcom-

90

ing the obstacles they encounter in achieving their dreams, goals, and objectives, your career or business will soar.

Challenges need to be embraced rather than avoided. (Read that again!) It is in the overcoming and teaching others to overcome that we grow and become the best we can be. The bigger the challenge, the bigger the opportunity for growth. There are some simple procedures positive producers can follow, which will enable them to overcome most of the challenges they are confronted with in their personal and professional lives.

Overcoming Challenges—*Step-by-Step*

Here are half-a-dozen ideas that can help you overcome challenges:

1. Get a complete picture of the challenge, including the good that will come out of it when handled properly. One example is improved relationships.

2. Pinpoint the specific challenge area(s).

3. Brainstorm your specific challenge area(s), and write down some solution ideas.

4. Give the analytical half of your brain time to compute the pros and cons of the possible solutions.

5. One to three days after your brainstorming session, analyze your best options while focusing on win-win solutions.

6. Choose what you believe is the best win-win solution and get behind it with dedicated, focused effort so you can make it work.

(•)*The first step you need to take is to get a complete picture of whatever challenge you are facing, including the good that will come out of it when properly handled. One example is improved relationships.* Let's say your challenge is that you didn't meet your organizational expansion goals during the past four months. For example, you didn't bring as many new people on to associate with you as desired. To analyze the situation, make a list of everything related to the success or failure of achieving that objective. You would probably note such things as meeting and befriending new people, sharing your product, service, or opportunity, leading people to associate with or buy from you, and continuing the relationships. By making an overview list, you get a complete picture of what you are dealing with. Then list the good to come out of overcoming the challenge—for example, improving your time and money situation, etc.

(•)*The second step is to pinpoint the specific challenge area or areas where you need strengthening.* Analyze each factor you listed in the previous overview phase of your challenge-overcoming process. Using our example, let's say that after careful analysis of all the factors, you look at the following:

1. The seriousness of your efforts to meet and befriend new people and, subsequently, to generate interest in your product, service, or opportunity.

2. The degree of discipline you demonstrated in following up with interested prospects.

3. The leadership ability, or lack of it, you showed in helping those people come on board as associates or clients.

4. Your caring enough about the people you are working with to help them in whatever way they needed assistance and encouragement from there on.

Perhaps you conclude that you need to be more alert to meeting new people everywhere you can. You might be fairly good at making friends but may lose focus when it comes to sharing what you have to offer. Therefore, you rarely even get to first base in expanding your business. Your analysis has narrowed the focus of the challenge. It is now limited enough for you to examine it thoroughly and correct it so you can move on.

(•) *The third step is to brainstorm about your specific challenge, and write down some solution ideas.* (If need be, ask your mentor or leader for help.)

1. Analyze it from both your viewpoint and that of potential prospects'.

2. Analyze it relative to how you are handling the situation and how successful leaders in your industry are handling it.

3. Compare your success at it now with your success at it a year ago, two years ago, or even five years ago. Are you improving? If not, is this maybe one of the reasons you might be stuck in your progress?

4. Take into account all the factors, some of which you need to deal with to reach your goal, that you may have carelessly ignored before now.

For example, one of your obstacles might be that you may always be going to the same places where you talk to the same people—passing the time. It may be a boring routine but you are used to it and in a comfortable rut. Your leader or mentor may have encouraged you to get out to new places and meet new people. You now realize that it's one of the things you need to do to accomplish your objectives.

Invest time analyzing yourself in relationship to the challenge: Do you believe you are too old or too young to make changes? Do you have a strong enough desire to change the situation successfully? Once you have concentrated on the many aspects of your specific challenge and, perhaps, consulted with or read about someone who has successfully overcome something like it, you will have a full range of ideas on which to base your responses. This will help you more confidently move forward.

• *The fourth step is to give the analytical half of your brain time to compute the pros and cons of the possible solutions.* You'll do this subconsciously. Before you begin your normal day or evening, pull out the notes you jotted down during your brainstorming session and read them over. At the end of the evening, read them again before you go to sleep. In between times, don't be concerned about making a conscious effort to overcome your challenge. Instead, each time your subconscious pops a possible solution into your mind, jot it down and save it. Give your subconscious mind time to analyze the full scope of the situation.

• *The fifth step is taken one to three days after your brainstorming session.* Analyze your best options, while focusing on win-win solutions. This requires compassion, understanding, humility, and forgiveness so you can heal any broken relationships that may exist. By now your subconscious mind will have come up with from one to four creative solutions. Using our business expansion challenge as an example, you may have had such responses as:

1. Strengthen your desire by focusing on your dream.

2. Make a list of opportunities to meet new people and schedule them into your planner.

3. Learn to meet new people and make more friends.

4. Explore continuing education opportunities in your industry to better prepare yourself to present what you have to offer in an appropriate, interesting way.

• *The sixth and final step is the most obvious one: Choose what you believe is the best win-win solution and get behind it with dedicated, focused effort so you can make it work.* Press forward with action, and have confidence in your ability to succeed while striving for an excellent result. But, if you don't attain it, keep going. At the very least, you learned what doesn't work and you can begin again, more intelligently, with increased vigor and renewed commitment. Remember, you will still be able to pull out your notes and have three other options to test. For the positive producer, the bottom line in all challenge-overcoming is to have faith and never, never give up.

Some equate an overload of stress with old-fashioned hard work. But the two are not the same. For positive producers, hard work doesn't lead to stress. They thrive on being productive; it's a reward in and of itself for them—it feels so invigorating and satisfying.

Boredom and Attitude, Not Stress, May Be the Challenge

Just as one person's junk is another's treasure, so, too, is one person's stress another's excitement. What may be agonizing drudgery to one may be fascinating and stimulating to somebody else.

Our attitude toward applying ourselves to achieve our dreams, goals, and objectives is the chief factor affecting how much stress or misery we may bring onto ourselves. Here's an example of something that occurred in my life which brought this whole matter of attitude into perspective for me.

A while ago, our church held a Mother-Daughter Banquet where the men were asked to serve as cooks and servers. I was assigned to wait on a table at which a dozen ladies were seated. For two hours, I took and placed orders, refilled water glasses, made trips back and forth to the kitchen, cleaned up spills, poured coffee, fetched extra napkins, carried hot dishes, and fixed clogged salt shakers. I asked "May I get you anything else?" often enough to sound like I was a stuck CD. At the end of those two hours, I was utterly exhausted. My legs ached, my perspiration-soaked hair was matted to my forehead, and my smile had changed to a snarl. I barely made it driving home without falling asleep at the wheel.

The next evening, I appeared as a guest speaker at a business dinner. Halfway through the meal, one of the servers tapped me on the shoulder, handed me a copy of my latest book, and asked me to autograph it. She said, "I admire you writers so much. Last week, I had to help my 12-year-old son prepare a two-page essay for his homework. What a struggle! I'm just no good with words. By the time we finally got it done, I had a headache and had to go to bed. I'd never make it as a writer. I need a simple ten-hour-a-day routine job like being a server where I don't have to do any heavy thinking."

My face paled. *Ten hours a day waiting tables?* Whew! The very thought of such a thing so soon after the previous night's events made me so tired I could barely rise from my seat to give the presentation. I had allowed that server to negatively affect my attitude. I vowed *never* to let that happen again.

Truly, attitude has everything to do with determining stress. I can recall times when I've worked at jobs I didn't like. I would come home ill-tempered, feeling worn out. All I could think of was taking a shower and going to bed early. Then, unexpectedly, a buddy of mine would call and ask if I wanted to join the guys at the gym for a few games of paddle-ball. Suddenly, I was pepped up and raring to go! It was all a matter of my attitude that either de-energized or energized me.

Since attitude toward work is so obvious a factor in business success, I have come to discount many of the so-called experts who say everyone who works hard experiences negative stress. Such opinions overlook something very important: Some people work hard because they enjoy working. *Not working* would be one of the most stressful developments that could occur in their lives!

The number of hours, alone, that we work has little to do with exhaustion and stress. But rather it's primarily a matter of attitude. Unfortunately, few people realize this. As a result, when they see someone who puts in a lot of hours, they say, "He's working his fingers to the bone"; or "She's going to work herself to death"; or "All work and no play makes Jack a dull boy." Why, instead, don't they say, "Susan is invigorated after engrossing herself in her business all evening," or "Mark has never been so fired-up building his business in the evenings and on weekends—working harder and longer than ever"? People typically relate work-hours to degrees of bodily exhaustion—but there is no such correlation! I can spend an eight-hour workday writing in my office and still feel refreshed; however, two hours of waiting tables leaves me physically and mentally drained. Time and manual output become insignificant factors in relation to stress when they are compared to our attitude toward work.

Relaxation Exercise

Here is a simple procedure which can be done at your work area, in an airplane seat, in a motel room, or even while seated in the most comfortable chair at home. Do it as often as you need to in order to release tension during your busy days and evenings.

1. Sit comfortably in your chair and put both feet on the floor. Shake your arms and hands a couple of moments so they are limp and relaxed, then rest your hands, palms-down, on your kneecaps.

2. Roll your eyes upward and keep them there as you close your lids.

3. Focus your attention on the ring finger of your right hand. Pretend a butterfly has a string tied from its legs to the finger and that as the butterfly rises and hovers four inches higher, it also lifts your hand. Let your hand stay in the air, floating in this relaxed position.

4. Imagine that it's a warm sunny day and you are strolling on the beach. Picture the scene, listen to the water as it gently laps the sand, and feel the warmth of the sun and deeply breathe in the salt-sea air.

5. Imagine a kind, friendly person smiling and walking toward you. When you meet, you tell your soon-to-be-new friend all about the most pressing situations bothering you at the moment. You begin feeling a sense of relief and even gain a new insight for addressing them. When you and your new friend part, you feel lighter, happier, and filled with more hope and anticipation than ever before.

6. Now slowly lower your hand. After a moment, feel free to open your eyes whenever you are ready. Tell yourself you now feel relaxed and refreshed.

Psychological Income

What, then, is the secret to being able to happily work 12 to 16 hours a day, all the while feeling energized and excited? The answer is *psychological income*—the return on your investment of time and energy (your work) which you receive in the form of recognition, compliments, influence, security, satisfaction, freedom, self-esteem, and new levels of achievement. Psychological income may be labeled by such catchwords as strokes and kudos, or by such traditional terms as praise and accolades. Whatever the expression, however, the bottom line still reads recognition, influence, and advancement.

We all like to be complimented. Getting a pat on the back, a nod of positive acknowledgment from the boss or leader, an achievement pin, or a trophy, ribbon, or plaque gives us a wonderful feeling that somebody cares—that we matter in the scheme of things. Some of us desire it more than others and are willing to work harder to gain it. Some of us yearn for the highest recognition (top income, most admired, or most honored reputation) and are willing to apply ourselves wholeheartedly to become unquestioned champions. In fact, most people will work harder for recognition than for money.

To those wanting psychological income, *not* endeavoring to be better than their best is far more stressful than applying themselves with unwavering dedication 15 hours a day. For example, General George S. Patton did not breathe a sigh of relief when he was pulled from command in 1943—he nearly went crazy with anxiety. Only when he was reassigned to a front-line command position in 1944, did he feel happy and content. He *wanted* the challenge; he *sought* the purpose of fighting for what he believed in; he *desired* the strengthening power of meeting and overcoming challenges.

Others have behaved similarly. Why have multimillionaires such as Roosevelt, Kennedy, Johnson, Reagan, and even George W. and George H.W. Bush sought a supposedly stressful job like the U.S. Presidency? For the salary? There's a laugh! No, it was for the psychological income—that sense of ultimate mission, accomplishment, influence, and usefulness. When someone attains a position like that, sleep often becomes a bothersome necessity. After all, it's much more enjoyable for the positive producer to stay awake and be the center of the action, taking every opportunity possible to make a meaningful contribution. We can all make a difference—big or small—in all areas of life—and leave a legacy.

I have a family physician whom I see once a year for a routine checkup. I just never seem to need him otherwise. Every time I go in for the checkup, he says, "Your weight is right, your lungs are strong, and your eyes are clear. You'd better keep coming in for the annual checkup however. We need to keep a watch on your heart."

"Why?" I ask. "Is something wrong?"

"No, not yet," he admits. "But as you get older, you may start to show some signs of stress and strain. I mean, it only seems logical at the rate you're going."

"What do you mean?" I ask.

"Well, you must never sleep. Nearly every day the newspapers contain articles written by you and I see you on TV regularly and the local bookstores are selling several of your books. Half the magazines in my waiting room have articles in them by you. No one can drive himself that hard and not put himself under a dangerous load of stress. Sooner or later, if you don't slow down, something's going to give."

This conversation has been repeated for 20 years now. But I still continue feeling great, have little need for a physician's care, and I continue working 10, 12, or more hours a day.

And why shouldn't I? For me, being a writer, teacher, and consultant is the greatest life I can possibly have. I love it. I truly, truly love it! I love to open the morning paper and see my byline on an important story and know that thousands of people may be reading *my words* right then. I love to receive regular phone calls that offer me all-expenses-paid trips to New York, Hawaii, or Hong Kong for a speaking engagement. I love to encourage people as I autograph books. And it's wonderful to board a plane and know I'm making a difference when I see someone reading one of my articles in a magazine.

These elements of psychological income, coupled with the never-ending opportunities to make a difference, are what make life thrilling for me. I never tire of such experiences. I never quit longing for them to be repeated. In fact, I work very, very hard so that they *will* be repeated. And my work serves as a joyful stimulus to the whole reward process. So, since I love my work and what it does for others, I do a lot of it. That, for me, is happiness and success.

Don't get me wrong though, I know it's not about me. Without the grace of God and help from a lot of other people, I wouldn't be where I am. But, fortunately, all things considered, I've been able to create a life I love, and you can too.

Every super-successful self-employed person I've ever met or read about has also had his or her "natural high" come in the form of psychological income. These men and women wear their honors like a general wears combat medals. In addition to becoming better than their own best, they relish the open competition for the position as top producer. They get excited about making presentations to share with others what they have to offer—regardless of the outcomes.

To garner such accolades, these entrepreneurs work diligently—concentrating on prospecting, communication and relationship-building skills, caring about others, focusing on objectives, short and long-range planning, business expansion, personal and professional development, giving and receiving mentoring, leadership skills, and whatever else it takes to be positive producers—while making a difference in their own ways. Their work is their pleasure. It manifests joy, not stress. It offers excitement, not drudgery.

If you are excited about building a business, don't let *anyone—especially yourself*—slow you down. Be your own judge of what is joyful work or stressful labor.

Maybe your job is what's stressful right now and others at work may be envious of your outside business activities. They would like to escape the rat race, too, but maybe aren't as committed to doing so as you are. So they may be warning you not to stress yourself out. Meantime, they are incredibly stressed out from the job and just trying to escape through entertainment activities. The reason you became an independent business owner, to begin with, was because you have a dream or goal to accomplish more in life, and you like the challenge and excitement of the work. Right? There's no reason for you not to maintain that original flush of enthusiasm. Stay psyched-up. It'll keep the stress away, and you'll be energized as you grow through the challenges—including the negativity of others.

Separating Psychological Income from Stress

If you have any doubts as to whether your long hours are motivated by enjoyment or pressure, use this quick true-or-false test as a guide:

1. I don't rely on stimulants or pills to keep me going.
   True False

2. I don't feel exhausted even though I sleep only five to seven hours a night.
   True False

3. I seldom suffer from headaches or backaches. **True** False

4. I pace and lead myself well. **True** False

5. I like and appreciate my mentor/leader, associates, clients, prospects, and corporate or other suppliers.
   True False

6. I am courageous enough to empower others to duplicate what I do. **True** False

7. I am motivated by the step-by-step accomplishment of my dreams, goals, and objectives. **True** False

8. I generously share what I have to offer and love making a difference. **True** False

9. I exercise daily and eat a healthy diet. **True** False

10. Getting a No may be a disappointment, but I just smile and say Next! **True** False

The more you are motivated by passion for what you are doing, the more true answers you'll have.

Overcoming the Perception of Inexperience

It can become challenging, at times, to stay psyched-up, especially if you're faced with what you consider to be a major situation to overcome. This is particularly true of people who have the heart and soul of a positive producer but who, because of their youth or inexperience, may find their credibility isn't great enough yet to gain the respect they desire. Fortunately though, there are ways of handling this challenge.

If you're a new or inexperienced business owner—you may have a challenge convincing certain people that you really know what you're talking about. For example, when you share an opportunity with an older, experienced schoolteacher and encourage her to follow your advice, she may say, "That's nice, but how successful are you?" Believe me, I know what that's like.

I've always had a boyish-looking face. Even today, I couldn't grow a beard if my life depended on it. When I enlisted in the Army, I was the only guy the medic gave a lollypop to when we got our shots. A woman asked me what I wanted to be when I grew up; she was my wife! We've been married for over 30 years, but each night at supper she still asks me if I want her to cut up my meat and potatoes—ahh, the price of a babyface.

Okay, so maybe I've been joking with you a bit. Still, I know that youthful looks can often be mistaken as a sign of inexperience, which can be a challenge for even the most energetic positive producer.

Truly, life has its ironies. When you're young and energetic and want prospects to take you seriously, they may be looking for someone more experienced. When you're older and more experienced, they may ask why you waited so long to contact them. It can be quite a challenge, but it can also be overcome. I've had some experience at this; so, let me put down my teddy bear and offer you five tips on how to overcome the look of inexperience:

1. Look the part.

2. Use official promotional/marketing materials.

3. Introduce your prospects to successful people in your industry with whom they can relate.

4. Exhibit an air of confidence.

5. Maintain a sense of urgency so prospects know you're moving on.

- *The first tip in overcoming the look of inexperience is to revamp your "look" as needed.* You need to look like you are in business, which can be done by following the recommendations and guidelines for your industry. It almost goes without saying that, first of all, cleanliness is an absolute and cologne needs to be used sparingly. For men, business attire may mean wearing a professional-looking suit (not necessarily expensive, but definitely clean and pressed), dark, shined shoes in good repair, a white or light-colored shirt, and a solid-colored (red is a nice power color) or conservatively patterned tie. Clean shaven is also recommended, since many people don't trust men with facial hair!

Women need to wear professional-looking modestly cut tops, shoes in good repair with no more than 2-inch heels, make-up which accents (not spotlights) your features, and conservative looking (no big dangling earrings) jewelry. The look of success boosts your credibility in the eyes of others—and in your own eyes as well!

- *The second tip in overcoming the look of inexperience is to use official promotional/marketing materials.* Hopefully you are fortunate enough to have a corporate supplier or leader who makes available official, product, service, or opportunity promotional and marketing magazines, brochures, videos/DVDs, audio tapes, CDs, or other such materials. Just be sure to follow your leader or mentor's recommendations and guidelines about sharing these items with prospective associates and clients. This helps give you a credibility edge, even if you are relatively inexperienced in your business, in that you are sharing quality material from a fine company or organization. Your success, whether you are seasoned or not, can be boosted by sharing such items for your prospects' review and consideration.

• *The third tip in overcoming the look of inexperience is to introduce your prospects to successful people in your industry.* Until you build your own credibility, it can be extremely helpful to introduce prospective associates or clients to successful people in your industry. Perhaps you have or can find a leader or mentor (which is good to do regardless of your experience or success) who is where you aspire to be in the business you're building. This individual would be more seasoned in your industry and more capable of fielding questions about whatever it is you're offering. He or she would also need to be supportive of you and the attainment of your dream, goal, or objective—generally or specifically speaking.

As you introduce your prospective associates to this person, be sure to appropriately and honestly share with the prospects, in a most complimentary way, how successful this leader or mentor is in your business and how it has enabled him or her to accomplish certain things like more time and money freedom. In addition, finding such credible people who also have a relatable professional history, that is, have followed a similar career path to the prospect prior to becoming successful in your business, can be particularly powerful.

For example, maybe you are looking to bring on an associate who is currently an attorney, which, as you probably know, is often a profession fraught with negativity. It could help immensely to introduce him or her to a successful former attorney in your business. Your prospect's ears are likely to perk up in response to the hope that the attorney gives by having been able to extract him or herself from that problem-filled legal role. This relatability/former-peer factor could play big in the prospect being excited about your business. It could be an important part of your prospecting strategy.

• *The fourth tip in overcoming the look of inexperience is to exhibit an air of confidence.* Always act confidently in front of prospects, associates, and clients. Keep your head up; look people straight in the eye; speak unhesitatingly in a steady rhythm; and stay calm when you are asked a question you cannot yet answer. Respond in a businesslike, humble, gracious, and accommodating manner, stating that you will be happy to do some research on that topic and will call back with a response. Have faith in the service, product, or opportunity you are offering and a belief in your abilities. You'll dramatically increase the chances that your prospects and associates will too!

Display an attitude of authority when dealing with your associates and prospects. When a physician examines your X-rays and says you will need to have surgery next Friday, you will most likely do what the physician tells you to do. Why? Because you respect his or her professional expertise. If you feel unsure, you'll get a second opinion.

When you develop a similar confident posture as a business person, while staying humble, it can work for you as well. If you are an insurance agent, you may need to say to your prospect, "Jim, you have a very nice family here. I'm sure those twin boys give you a lot of joy and satisfaction, and rightfully so. To provide for them properly, in the event you die before they grow up, you're going to need somewhere around $1,000,000 worth of permanent coverage. Let me show you why and then I'll show you how you can systematically work the premiums into your budget without a strain."

Even if you're relatively new at it, conveying an attitude that shows you are confident about what you offer with your business and directly recommending a policy amount, you sound like a professional. Your attitude conveys that you can help him or her. The prospect, in turn, feels more confident in dealing with you. He or she senses that you have things well in hand, and will listen more closely to the rest of your presentation. The same logic applies whether you are sharing an opportunity, selling skincare and cosmetics, telephone services, vitamins and food supplements, kitchen utensils, pots and pans, or something else.

• *The fifth tip in overcoming the look of inexperience is to maintain a sense of urgency so prospects know you're moving on.* After all, people will only follow someone who is going somewhere. Let them know you have a busy schedule, but you'll see what you can do to work them in. The idea that you are already moving on in your business, franchise, or company can do a lot to dispel the novice-like appearance that your youthful looks or lack of experience may engender.

Using any one of these tips will prove valuable to your success. Incorporating all five will almost completely negate any challenges you may have of appearing inexperienced or unqualified. Just be confident, enthusiastic, and passionate about what you're doing.

Getting More Appointments—*A Key to Greater Success!*

Another situation—one faced by both new and seasoned business people—is the challenge of setting up an appointment with an elusive prospect. But you *can* get that appointment when you give this challenge the same drive, energy, and patience you pour into any other worthwhile project. In my work as a reporter, I've had similar situations and have learned several effective ways to deal with them.

My colleagues—the other writers and journalists with whom I associate professionally and socially—call me the "luckiest doggone reporter" in the business. They say this because of my consistent ability to get interviews with famous personalities who are supposed to be impossible to interview.

But I scoff at the idea of luck playing any role in my success. If anything, I find the old adage, "The harder I work, the luckier I get," to be true. And because of working hard, I've been "lucky" enough to have had some dandy scoops during my career as a writer, including exclusive interviews with such personalities as Ed McMahon, Dolly Parton, Jane Seymour, Andy Griffith, Kenny Rogers, George Plimpton, and various other politicians, movie stars, generals, authors, and singers. Even as a young journalist, I landed some incredible scoops. I was the only reporter apparently persistent enough to interview Walter and Charlotte Baldwin, the father- and mother-in-law of the Rev. Jim Jones of the Guyana massacre. I was fortunate enough to be the only reporter to garner an interview with Dr. Ralph Honzik, the physician who was the campus director at Kent State University during the riots in which the National Guard shot four students.

My point in sharing these episodes with you is not to brag or even give you some insights into my career as a writer but, instead, to make a serious point about interviews and appointments: Whether you're a journalist, building a business, or advancing your career, the only interviews and appointments you fail to get are the ones you give up on.

Sure, I know you feel you have some solid reasons for why you weren't able to see So-and-So. But here's a list of some stock excuses:

1. "I couldn't get past her secretary."

2. "He's never in town long enough to schedule an appointment."

3. "I sent him a couple of letters and left several voicemails, but he just wouldn't respond."

4. "She told me 'no' a year or so ago, so there's no point in my trying to contact her again."

5. "He's so important that he probably wouldn't talk to me."

6. "She says she's too busy."

Sometimes these comments are legitimate—probably 20 percent of the time, I would guess. The rest of the time they are used as excuses to conceal the fact that we either lacked the nerve, the know-how, or the persistence to succeed in getting the so-called impossible-to-get appointment.

And let's face it, I had incentive: If you're a reporter and you can't get to newsworthy people for an interview, you're not going to wind up with salable articles and features. Similarly, if you're building a business and don't persevere until you get appointments to talk to potentially strong prospects, not much will happen!

Getting appointments is vital in business. And since the basics of getting interviews and appointments are similar, regardless of the reason for doing so, here's a list of four interview and appointment-getting strategies:

1. Keep yourself always ready to take advantage of chance opportunities to spontaneously talk with people.

2. Maintain your persistence and availability.

3. Connect with a third party who can intervene on your behalf.

4. Establish a chain of contacts who could lead you to the prospect.

• *The first strategy in getting more appointments is to always be ready to take advantage of chance opportunities to spontaneously talk with people.* As I mentioned earlier, I don't believe in luck. However, I do recognize the mathematical chance that two people living in the same area can be at the same place at the same time. When you have strong intention, focus, and a commitment to share what you're doing, coupled with the belief that you can do it, the possibility that you'll meet a prospect around town increases.

When you and your elusive subject happen to be at the same drugstore, grocery store, athletic event, or civic function, grab two minutes to extend the hand of friendship—and sincerely ask how things are going with the job, family, and such. People need to be cared about. When they sense you care about them, and show it by, for example, asking how his or her spouse is coming along after the operation, that elusive prospect can become a friend.

This was how I wound up with an interview with Dr. Ralph Honzik. He had not returned my calls or allowed his receptionist to schedule me for an appointment. Then one night, by chance, he and his wife attended a banquet my wife and I were also attending. I made sure that we sat near him, and, in time, I gave him my business card and a short list of references—names of editors he could ask about me. We got to talking and, before long, I had an appointment for the interview.

I never go anywhere without taking along the basic tools of my trade: a pen, pad of paper, business cards, and reference list. I'm always ready for opportunities whenever they present themselves. You need to do likewise. Carry plenty of business cards. Also, if your business has a recommended audio tape or CD, a brochure, or something else officially made to generate a prospect's interest in learning more about your product, service, or opportunity, be sure to carry these with you as you go about your activities.

In addition, always have your prospect list and contact information with you. Whenever you have a free moment, put a smile on your face, touch base with a prospect, see how that person is doing, and implement the approach you've been taught to get together with them.

Your constant preparedness and readiness for action gives you a decided edge. In a sense, you *make* yourself lucky. In truth, always carry your prospect list because the odds are against you running into some elusive person just by chance. It has happened to me only six times during the past 25 years. However, each time I was rewarded handsomely by being ready. I still go out prepared each day, expecting opportunity number seven to happen at any time!

(•) *The second strategy in getting more appointments is to maintain your persistence and availability.* You know the old adage, "If at first you don't succeed, try, try again." Well, it's a bit weak—*trying* doesn't make anything happen! *Doing* is what really counts, which is especially true when it comes to getting appointments. If you are rebuffed, it's your commitment that will win the day. You need to continue to endeavor to communicate. Show the prospect that you are excited and serious about wanting to talk to him or her. Don't depend on receiving a callback. It's your agenda and you need to be doing the calling.

Along with that, make yourself always available and ever adaptable to the prospect's personal circumstances. If you can't meet at one place, meet some place else—his or her home, the park, a nearby restaurant, a tennis club an hour before court time, or wherever. For the busy, elusive, or standoffish prospect who resists normal channels, innovative actions on your part are necessary.

I once interviewed Ed McMahon in the backseat of his car as he was being driven to the airport to catch a plane. I interviewed novelist Harry Mark Petrakis by following him to a book signing party and asking him questions between autographs. I interviewed the leader of a protest movement by walking around and around with her as she picketed a large corporation. These were not the techniques of interviewing I had learned about in journalism school. Be flexible and accommodating in pursuing out-of-the-ordinary people, and be persistent and ready to adapt to circumstances. Keep in mind that virtually no one asks you how long it took you to accomplish your goal; what matters most is that you *did.*

- *The third strategy in getting more appointments is to connect with a third party who can intervene on your behalf.* Many times your appointment candidate will sidestep you, ignore your calls, and continually refuse to acknowledge your efforts at communicating. That's when it may be time to involve a third party—someone who has influence with the person you want to talk to. It could be a person's spouse, a mutual friend, or someone else. Get to him or her and honestly explain why it could be beneficial to give you a chance to explain your ideas or talk about what you are offering. Sometimes this other person, who might be closer to your prospect, may say "John is really going through a tough time right now—he could use the opportunity you have." Ask this person if he or she could help you get the appointment.

Procedures which can aid in this process include offering the reluctant prospect some assurances, such as suggesting you won't need more than 20 minutes of his or her time. You may have other assurances that you don't expect him or her to make any decisions at lunch or that it won't affect your relationship if he or she isn't interested in what you have to share. The main point is that you need to give the third party something to take in with him or her when he or she intervenes to encourage the prospect to accept an appointment with you. In the process, who knows? The third party may be interested as well!

- *The final strategy in getting more appointments is to establish a chain of contacts who can lead you to the prospect.* For example, if you have a friend who has a neighbor who has a fraternity brother who is the cousin of the person you are trying to see, having successive communications with these people may be the best way of getting to see the prospect. As you share with these people to reach your prospect, you may even generate interest from *them* in what you have to offer! No matter what though, it is still up to you to schedule the appointment, unless someone is willing to do that for you, which could possibly happen. But they can, at least, potentially get you in contact with your prospect.

This is how I was able to interview Mr. and Mrs. Baldwin. After their daughter, Marceline, and their son-in-law, the Rev. Jim Jones, had drawn global focus because of the Jonestown, Guyana massacre, the Baldwins withdrew into their home and refused to talk to anyone. For ten days, reporters from TV networks, radio stations, and the print media congregated on the Baldwins' front yard, waiting for a public statement. It never came. At length, the FBI (Federal Bureau of Investigation) and local police dispersed the crowd. I then made *my* move.

I had taught a writers' workshop in the Baldwins' hometown about a year earlier, and I still had the list of my students. I began calling them to see if anyone knew the Baldwins or of someone else who did. After seven dead-end calls, I reached a former student whose husband had a boss who had a girlfriend who was the next-door neighbor of another daughter of the Baldwins. It took me about two weeks to get myself introduced to each person in that chain, but it got done! One afternoon, the Baldwins' daughter ultimately arranged for me to talk with her parents for 90 minutes at their home. For ten years, I generated articles based on that one in-depth interview. The same procedure can work for you in reaching elusive prospective clients. Just stick with it.

If you are having trouble getting appointments with two or three elusive prospects, use all four appointment-getting strategies. When you *are* able to land that so-called impossible-to-get appointment, you'll get a great morale and confidence boost and be able to move forward more quickly.

Life Is Full of Opportunities—*Disguised as Challenges*

We now see that becoming a positive producer can get us out of the doldrums and help us overcome many of our challenges. However, we are not starry-eyed enough to think that positive producers *never* have situations to deal with. They do. And when challenges arise, the confident, strong, determined positive producer is capable of facing up to any potential obstacle and working through it.

The way to overcome any challenge is to face it head on, get the true picture, break it down into specific, manageable pieces, and then pour your energy into overcoming it. When you are in better control of your life and enthusiastic about your career or business, you'll get stimulated and can work long and hard without becoming stressed out. You'll actually become more energized.

Some challenges seem monumental. Two of them include overcoming the perception of inexperience and landing appointments with elusive prospects. But even these situations can be approached and overcome in a systematic manner.

Strong-willed positive producers don't expect the game of life to be child's play, and they keep going—no matter what. After all, life is full of opportunities disguised as challenges. Its opportunities are for the taking; its challenges are for the meeting and overcoming. This is the only way we can grow and become better than we are, make our dreams come true, and successfully accomplish our objectives.

Some Thoughts About Work

"Don't loaf and invite inspiration; light out after it with a club, and if you don't get it you will nonetheless get something that looks remarkably like it. Work all the time."

—Jack London

"Keep away from people who try to belittle your ambitions. Small people always do that, but the really great make you feel that you, too, can become great."

—Mark Twain

"Love your work, your husband [or wife], and your child. If you wonder when you'll get time to rest, you can sleep in your old age."

—Beverly Sills

"Determine never to be idle. It is wonderful how much may be done if we are always doing."

—Thomas Jefferson

"Ah, but a man's reach should exceed his grasp, or what's a heaven for?"

—Robert Browning

"Nothing is particularly hard if you divide it into small jobs."

—Henry Ford

"*Positive productivity is a cure for challenges when it's embraced with the right perspective, considering one's dreams, goals, and responsibilities.*"

—Dennis E. Hensley

—6—

Positive Producers Need to Be Balanced and Understanding

"To be a successful positive producer, you need to be enthusiastic, optimistic, and imaginative, and have a good sense of who you are and what you have to offer."
—Dennis E. Hensley—

Since you've decided to become a positive producer and have begun acting like one, you might discover an occasional side effect. Positive productivity is like medicine—use the right dosage and you'll feel fine; take an overdose and you'll suffer.

There are some things you need to keep in mind. First, balance and blend your productivity with your personal life so you can avoid burnout. Second, if you are married, consider your spouse. Ask him or her to support you as much as possible with your career or business goals. Be patient and understanding if he or she doesn't always understand or agree with what you are doing. It can take a little while for some spouses to buy into what their partner is doing. Fortunately, proof of success will make the difference in most cases. Third, even though you are firmly focused on your goals, remember to be considerate of those around you—be sensitive to their concerns, ideas, plans, and opinions. By anticipating potential challenges, you can often prevent their development.

Burnout—*Symptoms and Cures*

We live in a fast-paced world. People used to wait three days for a stagecoach. But now, we jet around from one part of the world to another in less than a day.

Speed seems to be our primary concern. Fast-food restaurants, instant credit, one-hour photo shops, high-speed Internet, digital cameras, and microwave ovens are routine parts of our whirlwind way of life. Is it any wonder then that, from time to time, we may overload our mental and physical circuits and cause our own burnout?

Have you ever said, "I'm not as excited about my job as I used to be, and I don't seem to be getting anywhere"? If so, that's a possible sign of burnout. Have you ever asked, "Why am I always so tired?" or "What! Another staff meeting?" or "Who needs that client anyway?" These, too, are possible signs of burnout.

Burnout can sometimes become so advanced that it manifests physical symptoms such as insomnia, weight loss, headaches, backaches, nervousness, and exhaustion. It can also reveal itself in behavioral patterns like absenteeism, less concern for clients, associates, and prospects, overreacting to criticism and rejection, or making snap decisions about others based on limited knowledge. Left unchecked, this could lead to alcoholism, eating disorders, drug abuse, or marital and other relationship challenges.

To be a successful positive producer, you need to be enthusiastic, optimistic, and imaginative, and have a good sense of who you are and what you have to offer. Main tain a grip on the fact that life sometimes presents us with unexpected obstacles and is not always readily manageable. Handling life's surprises in a positive way is key to your well-being. Take the bitter with the sweet, look for the good and make something better out of it all.

Ten Remedies for Burnout

When you become aware of the signs of burnout, you can address the cause and either avoid or overcome it. Here are ten ways to reverse the feeling of being burned out:

1. Get adequate sleep and exercise daily.

2. Eat a balanced diet, maintain the proper weight, and take vitamins and food supplements.

3. Make positive use of your past and future.

4. Have something to look forward to.

5. Always be learning something new.

6. Say no when asked to do things that are out of line with your dreams and goals.

7. Travel more and expand your network of friends.

8. Make a habit of dreambuilding.

9. Set incremental, concrete goals, while keeping your plans flexible.

10. Regularly associate with caring, supportive people who are where you want to be and can offer you advice and encouragement.

• *The first thing you need to do is to maintain excellent health. This includes the items in one and two: get adequate sleep, exercise daily, eat a balanced diet, maintain the proper weight, and take vitamins and food supplements.* The body *requires* rest. It varies from person to person, but a minimum of six hours a day is recommended. Going to bed a little earlier, on occasion, taking a 20-minute power nap before or after dinner, and enjoying a long nap on free Sunday afternoons will give new vitality to your system. Similarly, a brisk half-hour walk in the morning, at lunchtime, or in the evening, will add stamina to your physical makeup. You may also want to consider other forms of exercise according to your doctor's recommendations.

The body requires food, the right kinds of food. Eliminate junk and fast food as regular fare, and follow your doctor's recommendations for a balanced diet. Obesity is a key health challenge that exacerbates any other health challenges you may have to deal with. Your doctor has a chart that can help you target your ideal weight. In addition to eating the right foods, be sure to take vitamins and food supplements as appropriate. Maintaining excellent health will enable you to handle stress much more effectively, and you'll feel better too!

• *The next two things you need to do are to make positive use of your past and future and have something to look forward to.* Keep a log of your greatest achievements in your business or career. Read it frequently and draw encouragement from past successes. Similarly, get into the habit of planning something to look forward to and be excited about.

Call a mentor, leader, or close friend who strongly supports you and set up a date for next week to get together to share dreams and goals. Provided your budget permits, schedule a day for fishing, hanging out at the beach, or doing something else fun before or after a weekend when you will be attending seminars held in resort or other interesting locations. And why not take your whole family along and enjoy the area together? Always have an anticipated event "carrot" dangling in front of you to help motivate yourself to achieve your objectives.

- *The fifth thing you need to do is to always be learning something new.* Mental stimulation is great for avoiding both depression and fatigue. Listen to educational and motivational tapes or CDs every day, and read an informative, inspiring book 15 to 20 minutes daily. Talk with people who care about you who are already savvy in what you're learning about and doing, and ask for their guidance. Challenge yourself to be a beacon of knowledge, and encourage others to do the same. You'll then open the door to work with others, multiply your efforts, and develop new prosperity. This will increase your enthusiasm for making things happen!

- *The sixth suggestion is for you to say no when you are asked to do things that are out of line with your dreams and goals.* As you've probably already discovered, you cannot be all things to all people! Beware of accepting more responsibilities than you have time to handle properly. You may have the short-term pleasure or relief of just saying yes but you will generate incredible amounts of worry, frustration, and stress, as well as disappoint yourself and others in the long-run.

When you are asked to handle something and you don't have the time to do so because of other priorities, be open and honest enough to say no. This gets easier the more you remind yourself that it is for your own good, as well as the good of whatever project someone is trying to get you involved in. Before long, you will be able to firmly, yet kindly reject such requests, as appropriate, without feeling guilty. In the long run, they'll understand as they realize the outcome benefits all concerned.

• *A seventh tip is for you to travel more and expand your network of friends in the process.* Burnout is sometimes caused by boredom which can be compounded by a lack of diversity in surroundings. If you have been reporting to the same office or doing business in the same area for a while, you may need to plan a change of place. For example, if your parents live out of town, before you go visit them the next time, make phone calls to seven families in the area and set up appointments to share whatever you're offering. (You might be able to get everyone together at your parent's home, at one time, which could be very efficient.) Get out and see new faces, travel new roads, eat in different restaurants. Keep busy expanding your web of influence. Keep in mind that in business expansion, variety is the spice of life.

• *An eighth idea is for you to make a habit of dreambuilding.* For example, your dream may be to build a new home. Go visit builders' shows and open houses offered by realtors. Take some business associates along and help them build their dreams too. It'll help you all bond, be more productive, and develop a sense of team, while building a brighter future together.

• *A ninth suggestion is for you to set incremental goals, while keeping your plans flexible.* Goal-setting is a must for anyone in business; however, if your goals are not attainable or your time-frame is unreasonably demanding, you will burn yourself out trying to reach it. Be more compassionate and flexible with yourself. Set goals which are challenging, but don't try to become financially independent in six months. You don't need that kind of anxiety or frustration. You'll make it in time. Be confident and just keep going—resetting your goals as needed. Change your plans as necessary, but stay the course.

• *The final tip is for you to regularly associate with caring, supportive people who are where you want to be and can offer you advice and encouragement.* Oftentimes, you can work with this group to reach similar goals and dreams. Such a support group can give you a better perspective on life, offer solutions to business and personal challenges, and provide opportunities for fellowship.

Everyone who works hard needs to guard against burnout. By incorporating some or all of the previously mentioned tips, you can pull yourself out of the burnout doldrums or, better yet, keep yourself from ever entering them.

Do Your Best to Include Your Spouse—*Ask for His or Her Support with Your Dreams and Goals*

Just as you can be faced with a challenge such as burnout, your wife or husband can become frustrated by similar situations brought on by your business. Be sensitive to his or her needs.

For example, I was invited to speak for a week at the University of South Florida, and my wife, Rose, flew down with me. After the first day, the university generously held a reception for me. One of the ladies who had attended my seminars on time management and freelance writing approached my wife.

"And you must be the poor dear who is married to this man who is always working," the woman said, half in jest, half seriously. "With as many books and articles as your husband has written, he probably never has time for you."

"Oh, quite the contrary," said Rose, casually. "In fact, he recently took me on a very nice vacation."

"Really?" said the woman, growing interested. "Where to? When?"

Rose smiled. "Florida...this morning."

That scene reminded me once again of how fortunate I am to be married to someone who knows how to live with and love a positive producer. My wife laughingly tells people that I'm hooked on my own adrenaline. If you are a successful entrepreneur, no doubt you are, and that's a wonderful thing—consider yourself blessed.

Since I love my career, I'm very happy when I'm working. You're probably the same way. Putting in a 10-, 12-, or even 15-hour workday is normal for us. Our spouses, however, unless they are joyfully working with us, may be far less exuberant about that. But since we love them even more than our career or business, it is our responsibility to help them learn how to live happily with us.

Here are several ideas you can suggest to your wife or husband to assist her or him in learning to live productively and joyfully with a dedicated positive producer.

• *Use the fun/work vacation plan.* By nature, positive producers often loathe vacations—it keeps them away from their beloved work! The thought of sharing a lonely mountain lodge with friends for a week of relaxation and nature hikes is enough to cause a positive producer to experience cabin fever. We need work the way an eagle needs to fly—we can't stay away from it for very long.

Still, we all (yes, even positive producers) need occasional short vacations and rest periods. The solution my wife and I have developed is a fun/work vacation plan. When she and I fly out of state for a few days of fun, she says nothing when I put in a couple of hours of work in the morning, which could be writing, appearing on a TV talk show, or giving a presentation at a convention. After that, we spend the rest of the day together shopping, sightseeing, or doing something else relaxing and fun.

Before they were grown, we used to take our two children with us and reverse the order of the day's activities. First, we would have our family fun together until 3 p.m. After that, I would put in a few hours of work, while Rose and the kids went to a movie or took a swim in the motel pool. Rather than *criticize* me for not "letting go" completely while on vacation, my wife *thanks* me for bringing her along on so many wonderful trips.

To prevent feeling uneasy during vacations, keep them relatively short, and blend them with a business or seminar trip as discussed earlier. Or you could use the same fun/work plan, or the reverse of it, as need be. Each morning, you could make calls to prospects, associates, or clients, or you and your spouse could invest time reading some good, positive business-related or personal development books, or both of you could have breakfast with a new prospect. After a couple of hours of work, your work-related conscience would be at ease and your readiness for fun would be at a peak. You will feel as though you have earned it.

My wife and I are both active and involved in our separate careers and interests while maintaining our mutual devotion to each other, our children, and the church. In your case, your spouse may desire to be more than a sideline observer. So suggest some ideas for ways in which he or she can participate in your business activities.

- *Let the money you earn benefit you both.* Some positive producers continue working 12 or more hours a day, long after any financial challenges have been overcome. And even though they are more prosperous, they continue as if they were still broke when, in truth, they could well afford to realize some dreams.

I used to be that way too. Then, one day, my wife said she wanted a new computer, but I said we couldn't afford it. I was just so used to the days when we were first starting out and had little money that I had lost sight of the fact that we could now afford to treat ourselves more generously.

"Look," said my wife, "You're working 12 or more hours a day, Monday through Saturday, and earning more money than we ever imagined. If we can't afford some nice things by now, we never will. So, what do you think about freeing up some funds?"

The next day we bought a new computer. Shortly after that, we bought a new car! She had been right. Anyone willing to live with a positive producer's crazy hours, schedules, and habits—once the prosperity level makes it possible to do so easily with cash—deserves to benefit from that person's efforts. Fair is fair. After all, what are you working for? Positive producers love to work, but as their financial picture brightens, they need to remember that they are also working to achieve dreams and goals—not only for themselves, but for their families as well.

- *Have frank discussions.* Positive producers are single-minded, determined, and purposeful—but that doesn't mean they're always right. I know I'm not. I sometimes fall short of the mark, no matter how good my intentions are. Fortunately, though, my wife has enough sincere concern for me to point out, in a direct but loving way, the areas where I need to improve. By being open-minded and respectful of what she says, I've learned a lot and avoided some potential challenges.

My wife and I often engage in frank discussions. We see nothing productive in sulking, ignoring each other, or displaying pig-headed obstinance. As such, we strive to clear the air whenever something bothers either of us.

I'm not saying it's a joyful event when my wife tells me I need to lose ten pounds, or that I'm spending too much time listening to my college students talk about their writing projects and not enough time writing myself. Still, it's the best way to handle a positive producer—straightforwardness is essential. Since a positive producer's mind is often racing, being subtle isn't effective. Besides, getting to the point right away saves time. Positive producers *love* to save time!

So take an hour or two and encourage your spouse to really talk to you. If it turns out that, in your hustle and bustle, you've forgotten to give flowers on an anniversary, or your constant use of his or her favorite car has become a selfish habit, or you haven't been paying him or her enough attention, sincerely apologize, then start to make amends. Evict your ego so you aren't blinded to your faults. Listen, always be humble, accept responsibility for your behavior, and keep those conversational channels open. This goes a long way in creating and maintaining a happy marriage.

• *Use time-saving devices.* Positive producers tend to put people on their *own* schedule rather than adapt to the schedules of others. This is egocentric and arrogant, and reflects an attitude of "It's all about me"—which is extremely ineffective in building a win-win marriage, or any kind of relationship for that matter. It's also detrimental to our children or a spouse with a full-time job.

One of the ways to get around this, however, is to take greater advantage of the machines and electronic devices readily available so you and your spouse can make the best use of time.

If you'd like to ask your spouse to join you for a business meeting or presentation when he or she typically washes the dishes, you might want to consider investing in a dishwasher. If you want to ask your spouse to help you with some calls this evening, but the car needs to be washed and waxed, you could go to a drive-through car wash on your way home from work. The same work will get done as always, but it will be done by machines, and in less time. Work smart—not just hard.

• **Establish roles.** Many positive producers assume they have to do *everything* themselves in order for things to be done right. But a perfectionistic attitude can be extremely offensive to a spouse. Instead, the positive producer needs to respect and encourage the spouse to handle that person's share of the responsibilities.

At one time, I was holding down two jobs while also completing my Ph.D. in English, and I had to give up various responsibilities at home. So I asked my wife to handle certain things I had been doing. She met the challenge very well. Although she is somewhat shy, I've nudged her into such things as negotiating a bank loan, purchasing investment notes, and working on our tax forms. She feels as vital and useful to the family as I do...because she *is*!

• **Ask for business-related assistance.** You know that old line that goes, "If you can't beat 'em, join 'em." As a positive producer, you could reverse that adage and make it, "Since you can't change my commitment to my business activities, then you might as well join me."

That has worked for me. If I'm rushed to meet a deadline, my wife will often help me with my computer chores. If I need a second opinion on something I've written, she'll read it and offer revision suggestions. If I'm short on time in completing a research project, she'll go to the library or online to get the information for me. This not only helps her keep aware of the projects I'm working on, but also provides a way for us to be together and work as a harmonious team.

Your spouse could discover how much fun it is to be a positive producer and develop a new spark of interest in working with you in your business. He or she could simply ease into it. For example, if you need someone to listen to your presentation and offer constructive comments, kindly ask your spouse to play the role of prospect. Also, you may have a local business meeting one evening that you and your spouse could attend together. He or she may begin to enjoy your associates and what you are doing more quickly than you might expect. Introduce him or her to an associate who has something in common. For example, if you have kids, introduce her to another mom! Give your spouse a chance.

Your spouse may not feel welcome in your arena because you have been so busy running off to business-related activities *alone*. You may not have suspected that your spouse felt left out and has been wishing you would extend an invitation to join you! (Even kids can participate—for example, by answering the telephone and doing age-appropriate tasks. Just ask. You may be surprised.)

Spouses who work together usually say that it is the best thing they do to strengthen and harmonize their marriage. It causes them to work through issues they had ignored before—otherwise they couldn't be as productive together. Each truly understands what the other is going through every day because they both have a pulse on and are contributing to the success of the business. They have the same dreams, goals, and friends, and are engaged in overcoming the same challenges. This not only serves to strengthen their bond, but also helps them move ahead in business as well as in life.

Two of my friends always say, "We got married to be together." They just love working with each other in their home-based business. They travel—happily blending work and play everywhere they go. Positive productivity courses through every vein in their bodies!

When you consider ways to ask your spouse for help, think of the great opportunities you'll have to do more things together. Be encouraged even if your spouse doesn't want to help you with your business right now. He or she will most likely want to participate later as your attitude, enthusiasm, and success increase. Perhaps when your spouse observes how much fun you're having, the new friends you're making, and that you're substantially increasing your income by doing it, this could be the catalyst for such a change.

• *Turn criticism into mutual appreciation.* Positive producers, until they involve their spouses and kids in their business, will, at least temporarily, deprive their families of some of their time. And they may be criticized for it. Remember, however, that all efficient positive producers, in the long-term, provide many spin-off benefits for their family members which other families are not privileged to receive. It's good to remind your spouse of such benefits.

So, for example, as your positive productivity results in more financial freedom, which, of course, benefits the family, remind your spouse of it. Also, thank him or her for any support you received in the process.

No one gets a free ride in life—especially entrepreneurs. As you achieve more success in your business, you will probably receive greater respect from your family. To encourage that, readily show the correlation between your positive productivity, your vision of a better life, and your ability to provide for your family. They might complain in the beginning, but keep persisting with what you know you need to do, and the rewards will come for everyone.

• *Coordinate scheduling.* I mentioned previously that my wife and I arrange working vacations for ourselves during the year. We also do a lot of other coordinated scheduling. For example, if she wishes to travel 350 miles to her father's home for a weekend, I arrange to hold a book autograph party in a local bookstore in that town. If she wants to visit friends in a distant town, I take along my camera and notepad and work on a feature article about some celebrity or special landmark in that area.

Coordinate your calendar so you can make the best use of your time. For example, if your wife wants to take a little vacation, suggest holding off until the week you are going away for a business convention in a major city, and then take her along. Make an agreement that she join you at the convention, if allowed, and enjoy the sights with you during free time or after it's over. The more you coordinate your schedule with your spouse's, the more you'll be able to continue your work—doing it together to whatever degree you can—and not be apart.

• *Give in—on both sides.* My mother used to tell me that marriage harmony was a 60/40 plan. Each spouse gives in 60 percent of the time and holds the line 40 percent of the time. Years ago, when I first heard that, I thought it was just a cute comment. Today, after over 30 years of marriage, I know—it's really true!

Both the spouse and the positive producer (hopefully the spouse will become a positive producer as well!) need to develop mature love, which includes, among other things, patience, tolerance, respect, gratitude, a giving, positive frame of mind, flexibility, and appreciation for the other person. Before each comments about the other's habits, attitudes, or behaviors, each needs to do his or her best to understand the reasons behind such developments.

Focus on arriving at a win-win situation rather than just criticizing and creating resentment and a stand-off. Focus on establishing alternatives rather than arguments. Focus on establishing family peace rather than inciting a family debate that keeps the disagreement alive rather than resolving it. Agree to disagree on certain matters where agreeing isn't essential for family harmony.

Success in business is of less value if you fail on the home front. It's great to be a positive producer and don't let anyone tell you otherwise, as the rewards can be awesome. But always do your utmost to be understanding of your spouse's concerns, know what you're working for and why, and stay focused.

Burnout and spouse alienation are two of the most common situations that could be encountered by positive producers. But as we have just observed, they can be avoided altogether or, at least, overcome.

Positive productivity is a cure for challenges when it's embraced with the proper perspective, considering one's dreams, goals, and responsibilities. It is not meant to be a creator of challenges, but rather a wonderful way to grow and overcome them. Let positive productivity work for you by doing your best to be balanced and understanding.

"When you work to make your dreams come true, coupled with the noble and rewarding focus of reaching out and helping others, you are doing the right thing and working for the best reasons."

—Dennis E. Hensley

"*When our attitude is right about doing good work, as we build our business or career, and our actions reflect our attitude, our work is outstanding. A proper attitude, when habitual and fueled by our dream, goal, or objective is a natural incentive for a positive producer.*"

—Dennis E. Hensley

The Natural Incentive to Be a Positive Producer

"Confidently say, 'I can do anything. I just need to find value in it and excitement for it. After that, my enthusiasm and steadfast commitment will propel me to do the rest.'"
—Dennis E. Hensley—

Henry J. Kaiser, the great steel and aluminum magnate, said, "When your work speaks for itself, don't interrupt."

Kaiser was a man who, quite obviously, knew why some of us choose to work very hard. He knew that work well done offers a reward beyond measure, beyond accolades; that reward was and still is deep personal satisfaction and a gratifying sense of meaning. Feeling good about doing fine work which contributes to society and makes a difference provides a natural incentive for working hard and completing each business activity at hand. When you work to make your dreams come true, coupled with a noble and rewarding focus of reaching out and helping others, you are doing the right thing and working for the best reasons.

You've discovered the many benefits of being a positive producer. We've noted that the consistently dedicated positive producer obtains financial security and freedom, increased respect, greater admiration and influence, more professional distinction, heightened family support, cooperation and harmony, as well as additional free time.

All of these benefits are certainly worth pursuing and having but, once again, they pale in comparison to the greater foundational, day-in-and-day-out benefit of personal growth and fulfillment. There is nothing more pleasurable than enjoying what we do, and knowing, without being told, that our performance is outstanding.

There is something inherent in each of us that tells us we need to feel morally and ethically responsible to perform to the highest possible degree of excellence. You may have grown up hearing your parents say something like, "If something is worth doing, it's worth doing well." I would add to that by saying, "If something is worth doing, it's worth doing poorly until we can do it well." When our attitude is right about doing good work as we build our business or career, and our actions reflect it, our work is outstanding. A proper attitude, when habitual and fueled by our dream, goal, or objective, is a natural incentive for a positive producer.

How about you? Do you have a winning attitude? It'll be to your benefit. Begin now by confidently saying, "I *can* do anything. I just need to find value *in* it and excitement *for* it. After that, my enthusiasm and steadfast commitment will propel me to do the rest." An attitude of strength and confidence leads to behavior which exhibits strength and confidence. When you *believe* that nothing can thwart your good work, and your actions demonstrate that this is so, then nothing will be able to stop you. You'll go under, over, around, or through any obstacle that may threaten to stop you—or you'll eliminate it all together. You'll steadfastly hang in there, persistently doing what you need to do, until the last bell is rung.

Never let your winning attitude be modified or hampered in any way, even if your dream or goal seems unreachable. Having nothing to do and no one relying on you is far worse. Charles Kingsley admonished, "Thank God every morning when you get up that you have something to do that day which *must* be done, whether you like it or not. Being forced to work and do your best will breed temperance and self-control, diligence and strength of will, cheerfulness and contentment, and a hundred virtues which the idle person will never know." Positive producers don't let circumstances hold them back because they are drawn forward by their dreams.

The right attitude will help you achieve greatness in spite of any challenges, setbacks, or shortcomings that may be encountered. I once interviewed country music singer Ronnie Milsap, who was born blind. He shared that his career as a singer and pianist was a series of disasters—one failure after another—during his early years. Then one day in Memphis, Tennessee, he had the opportunity to meet the late great blues artist Ray Charles.

Milsap told Charles that he had emulated him all his life. He sang like him, played like him, and performed like him; still, he had never achieved success. Charles then stunned Milsap by saying that he felt Ronnie had the wrong attitude: "By copying me, you are saying you have no confidence in your own musical style," he told Milsap. "I became successful by believing in myself. You need to do the same thing. Change your attitude about yourself."

Milsap heeded those words. He stopped imitating Ray Charles's rhythm and blues style and, instead, began exploring the country music of his own heritage. Within four years, Milsap was nominated for the Country Music Association's "Entertainer of the Year Award." Confidence and the right mental attitude had made all the difference in Ronnie Milsap's career.

I once wrote a series of articles about a man named Pete Schlatter. Pete was partially crippled by polio when he was a child. Because he could not run, skip, jump, and climb as other youngsters could, he became very dexterous with his hands. People called him a "tinkerer" and his parents encouraged him to read about motors, electrical circuits, and machinery.

As a boy, Pete loved to read the "Smokey Stover" comic strip. Smokey was a humorous fire chief who rode in a wonderful two-wheeled automobile. Pete told his parents and friends that, one day, he was going to invent a *real* car that would look and run just like Smokey Stover's. Everyone smiled patronizingly; some even tried gently to explain that it was impossible for a car to run on two wheels because it would not be able to balance itself.

But each time someone chided him about his dream, Pete became all the more determined to prove he could build the "impossible" two-wheeled car. He even wrote to William Holman, creator of the "Smokey Stover" cartoon strip, to see if anyone else had ever tried to build the two-wheeled car. Holman wrote back to say that, over the course of 20 years, three teams of engineers had tried and failed. Nevertheless, even this did not discourage Pete.

For years and years, Pete Schlatter spent his spare time working to invent a workable two-wheeled car. Although Pete became successful as a farm machinery designer and an engine repair expert, he still measured his success in life by how close he came each year to inventing a two-wheeled car. He was out to prove something to himself. This internal quest, his dream, helped him maintain an attitude of strength and confidence, and gave him the natural incentive to keep going.

By the time he was 50 years old, Pete had developed more than two dozen prototypes of the two-wheeled car, and each had failed. Then, one summer, Pete produced a two-wheeled car that was almost perfect. It weighed only 850 pounds, could go up to 25 miles per hour, and was able to get 30 miles per gallon of gas. Its only flaw was that whenever it made a very sharp turn, it would fall forward onto its hood and front bumper.

"I was disappointed, naturally," said Pete. "I was so close, yet not close enough. For me to know, personally, that I had achieved my goal, the car would have to work perfectly."

But then, Pete's breakthrough finally came about. As he explained it, "One of my friends asked me if this latest failure had taken the wind out of my sails [discouraged me]. Bingo! That gave me an idea. I rushed back to my garage, put oversized radial tires on my little car, and let out one-third of the air in each one. I got in, took off...and the car worked perfectly! The flatter tires provided just enough extra support to keep the car balanced, even during turns."

Pete's dream came true. And it made him famous and financially independent. Orders for his little cars came in from everywhere—Hollywood movie producers wanted them for stunt scenes; golf course owners wanted them for unique golf carts; and rodeo clowns wanted them for comedy routines. Pete's car was featured in the automotive section of a major national newspaper (I wrote the story!) and in numerous newspapers and trade magazines, including *Mechanics Illustrated*. It was displayed nationwide at auto shows and shown on TV-news programs.

Sure, Pete Schlatter gained fame and fortune by creating the two-wheeled car. But he will tell you he gained more than that; he realized something of far greater value—personal growth and a deep sense of accomplishment. Every time Pete drove his little two-wheeled car in a parade or stood by it at an auto show, he experienced a wonderful sense of accomplishment which only a positive producer who has overcome the odds can know. Pete Schlatter invented the two-wheeled car...because it was important for *him* to know he could do it. He set his own goal, mastered his own destiny, and lived up to his own high standards. Through it all, his winning attitude fortified him.

The right attitude can also help you overcome any personal challenges others (or you, yourself) may think you have. Blindness couldn't stop Ronnie Milsap; polio didn't stop Pete Schlatter; being short didn't stop Napoleon; being partially bald didn't stop General Douglas MacArthur; having a large nose didn't stop Jimmy Durante; losing an eye didn't stop Moshe Dayan; being a stutterer didn't stop W. Somerset Maugham; not finishing college didn't thwart Bill Gates, and having only three months of school didn't stop Edison. All positive producers know how to stay the course and don't let challenges that side-track average-thinking people thwart their efforts.

Lord Chesterfield advised, "Know the true value of time; snatch, seize, and enjoy every moment of it. No idleness, no laziness or procrastination: Never put off till tomorrow what you can do today." Charles Lindbergh shared, "It is the greatest shot of adrenaline to be doing what you've wanted to do so badly. You almost feel like you could fly without a plane." On that same note, Helen

Keller noted, "One can never consent to creep when one feels the impulse to soar." Proverbs 10:4 expounds, "Lazy hands make a [person] poor, but diligent hands bring wealth." Henry David Thoreau wrote, "What people say you cannot do, you try and find that you can."

Throughout the ages, philosophers and historians have all noted that nothing is as valuable as a confident, persevering, goal-oriented achiever. In this book, we have seen how a positive approach to our business or career can strengthen us physically, mentally, and spiritually; and we've seen how our positive productivity can provide benefits for our family and many others whom we serve. Knowing all this gives us a natural incentive to want to be peak performers, achieve our dreams and goals, and make a difference.

The opportunities to stretch your wings and fly like an eagle are endless and ever present. Starting today, know that you are now a dynamic, ever-growing positive producer. Watch, with amazement, as you soar ever upward. The clouds that were once in your way will part, and you'll fly where even eagles have not dared to go. Pass through these life-changing portals into the new realm of positive productivity, and be the joyful, successful person you were created to be. You can do it!

Who Is Dennis Hensley?

Dennis E. "Doc" Hensley is an author, speaker, and consultant. He holds four degrees in communications, including a Ph.D. in English, of which he is a professor at Taylor University's Fort Wayne, Indiana campus. He has been director of the professional writing major there since he created it in 1997.

Doc also teaches courses in public relations, professional writing, corporate communications, and investigative journalism. As a consultant, his clients include Wells Fargo, Chrysler Corporation, North American Van Lines, Raytheon Corporation, Waterfield Mortgage, Lincoln Life Insurance Company, and numerous others.

Doc has written six novels, eight text books on writing, more than 150 short stories, and 45 other books on topics such as time management, motivation, Christian doctrine, and public relations.

Doc was named a "Distinguished Alumnus" of Saginaw Valley State University and T.L. Handy High School. He received the "Award for Teaching Excellence" from Indiana University and was also presented the "Dorothy Hamilton Memorial Writing Award."

Doc and his wife Rose, who reside in Fort Wayne, have two grown children, Nathan and Jeanette.